T0113810

THE Keys TO THE KINGDOM

BOOK ONE:

Love

Baron Stepney *and* Robert M. Paris

WESTBOW
PRESS®
A DIVISION OF THOMAS NELSON
& ZONDERVAN

This book is a work of non-fiction. Unless otherwise noted, the author
and the publisher make no explicit guarantees as to the accuracy of
the information contained in this book and in some cases, names
of people and places have been altered to protect their privacy.

Scripture taken from the New King James Version. Copyright © 1979, 1980,
1982 by Thomas Nelson, Inc. Used by permission. All rights reserved.

Scripture taken from the King James Version of the Bible.

WestBow Press books may be ordered through booksellers or by contacting:

WestBow Press
A Division of Thomas Nelson & Zondervan
1663 Liberty Drive
Bloomington, IN 47403
www.westbowpress.com
1 (866) 928-1240

ISBN: 978-1-5127-3999-2 (sc)
ISBN: 978-1-5127-4000-4 (e)

Library of Congress Control Number: 2016906800

Print information available on the last page.

WestBow Press rev. date: 04/22/2016

CONTENTS

INTRODUCTION

If you believe in Jesus Christ, this book contains breakthrough revelation that will catapult your spiritual growth. It is designed to meet you wherever you may be in your walk; at whatever stage you are in, or whatever level you may be on. The condition of your heart will determine the degree of truth you are able to perceive (or the amount of Himself God allows you to glimpse).

This book is the Holy Spirit's work. None of the events, themes, or teachings in The Keys to the Kingdom of God were altered or inspired by our creativity in anyway. We wrote exactly what He taught us, exactly how He taught us. The Holy Spirit instructed us to emphasize that He wrote this!

We believe that the body of Christ (i.e. the church) has been in a building, growing, 'discipleship' phase since our Master's ascension. In "The Great Commission," Jesus mandated the apostles to "make disciples"- not "apostles." In other words, they were not sent to necessarily graduate the students (i.e. disciples), only gather them. We believe that the entire body has entered a pivotal transition phase. God is about to finish what He started.

He always intended to multiply His only begotten Son into "sons."

Jesus was the greatest Man to ever walk this earth. The single most powerful, life-changing, divisive, and impactful figure in all of history. When He sacrificed His life, He left behind a handful of trained apostles who moved in this same capacity; with the same characteristics and capabilities. They preached the gospel of Jesus, spread the good news of God's kingdom, and displayed God's power through signs and wonders. These men turned the world upside down, and it has never been the same. Now, if twelve fully developed, empowered, anointed and appointed men of God could do that, imagine 1,000! Imagine 100,000! Imagine 1,000,000!

This is the vision that God gave us.

Brothers and sisters in Christ, He is calling us to another dimension in Him. Our heavenly Father is calling us higher. And He is calling us closer; closer than we've ever been. If you feel like there is more- you are right. There is so much more. We hope and pray that you are ready for The Keys...

CHAPTER 1

Baron and Rob had both been incarcerated in the Feds for years. Baron was at U.S.P. Hazelton, West Virginia, and Rob was at U.S.P. in Lompoc, California.

After being at an institution for a certain amount of time, you could have your counselor submit the paperwork to be transferred to another facility. Being so many miles away, they both dreamed of the day when they would get an opportunity to be transferred closer to home. Namely F.C.I. Butner- the only federal prison complex in the state of North Carolina where they were both from. The chances were slim because almost all federal prisoners from North Carolina tried to get to Butner, but they were both accepted and designated to be transferred there in the spring of 2013.

They were flown to the national federal transit center in Oklahoma, and then flown into the nearest airstrip to Butner, N.C. They were transported to F.C.I. Butner by bus, fed and processed. It definitely wasn't freedom, but they felt real good to be "back home." Things seemed to be getting better.

They were allowed to shop at the prison's commissary that following Monday. Rob had already shopped and was sitting on a bench waiting on a move (designated times where inmates were allowed to travel from one area to another) when Baron approached. He sat his bag on the ground and took a seat beside Rob.

"What's up, man?" Baron greeted Rob and extended his hand.

"What's good?" Rob replied and smiled in recognition of the slim, light brown-skinned guy with dreads that arrived with him days ago. He shook his hand.

"I see you bought some food and stuff."

"Yeah, man, I am trying to get situated."

"Yeah, I got a few items myself.They've got some stuff here that... they didn't have at the spot I left."

"Where are you coming from?" Rob asked.

Baron gazed off as he shook his head in regret at the long season of his life spent imprisoned in the mountains of West Virginia. He snapped out of it, smiled and sighed. "Man, they had me way in West Virginia- Hazelton. Boy! I'm glad that chapter's over! What about you? Where are you coming from?"

"I'm coming all the way from the west coast- Lompoc, California."

"Wow, man!" Baron exclaimed in shock. "They had you way on the west coast?!"

"Yep," Rob replied, this time shaking his own head in disbelief. "They had me at the ends of the earth!"

"That's crazy. Well, at least we're back in N.C. now."

"Yeah, glad to be back, too. I've been a thousand miles away for too many years."

"Who are you telling? Hey, didn't I see you in church Sunday?" Baron asked.

"Yeah, I was there."

"How'd you like it?"

"It was good. Haven't been to a service like that in awhile," Rob answered.

"Yeah, me neither. The church where I just left was dead. I felt the Spirit in there Sunday, though. It felt good, too."

"Yeah, well, the church where I left had good preaching, but didn't have much of a worship service. That service Sunday really moved my spirit."

Baron sighed, smiled and glanced off to the side, "Are you a Christian?"

Rob replied with firm conviction, "Yeah. I'm a Christian," and nodded his head.

"I mean, are you a...REAL Christian?" Baron asked and looked at Rob suspiciously.

Baron had met many Christians over the years since his conversion. They fell into a slew of different categories, and though he was far from self-righteous he'd yet to meet many whom he considered "real" Christians, or ones he felt matched his drive, dedication and passion for God. It wasn't that he felt like those whom lacked his fire weren't genuine and sincere; he knew that only God could see the hearts of men. But he just had a higher regard for men who hungered for the things of God as he did.

"Yeah, I'm a real Christian! What do you mean a REAL Christian'?" Rob shot back, sensing what Baron was getting at but shocked that his own dedication was in question. He, too, shared the experience of fellowshipping with few brothers who matched his zeal.

"I go hard," Baron said and smirked, "Like- I go hard for my God."

"I go hard, too!" Rob exclaimed, eyes bulging.

Baron laughed and threw his hands up in mock surrender to calm and disarm Rob. "Hey, man, I'm not trying to attack you. I just needed to know."

* * *

(U.S.P. Hazelton)

Baron's growth had been gradual yet consistent over the years. The first thing that he asked the Lord to take from him was foul language. That had been immediately, right in the beginning of his walk, and had not been hard for him to overcome. This was while he was still in the county jail awaiting sentencing.

When he first got to prison his church attendance started off regular, but the lack of spirit-filled worship or preaching at the services left him feeling emptier and more drained than anything. He knew back then that God dwelled within His people and that "the church" was not a building, so he didn't like the feeling of going to church services out of obligation. Eventually his attendance waned.

He drank wine (prison-brewed hooch) from time-to-time, smoked weed on his birthdays and entertained his lusts all in what he considered was moderation. That's how he justified all of his indulgences- he told himself that he was just remaining grounded and not being extreme. He'd heard the cliché that some became "so heavenly that they were of no earthly good," and he did not want to fall into that holier-than-thou stigma.

He continued in this state for the next six years- believing in Jesus yet practicing his own form of Christianity while remaining powerless, uninspired, and spiritually ineffective and stagnated. He wore his religion on his sleeve and was respected in the penitentiary as both a solid convict and Christian, but he secretly yearned for God to show up and fulfill the promises He had made to him.

His commitment and spiritual state gradually grew weaker. Then things in his personal life went bad. Then they got worse. Baron always had his private, personal goal of stepping up and improving his personal walk when he turned thirty. The Bible said that Jesus began His ministry at around thirty years of age, and he always imagined being empowered along the same timeline.

He was in the shower one night and his sorrows overcame him. He became desperate. He was desperate for his freedom, desperate for help and change. He was desperate for God- for God to move. With everything going so bad and his thirtieth birthday looming, Baron made his decision. He made his decision to completely surrender. His decision was to give God whatever He required in exchange for His power; His hand; His aid.

He was desperate for God to do something. He wanted to be home with his daughter and fiancé more than anything. In his desperation- his brokenness- he determined that the cost no longer mattered. He would sacrifice today- and however many more were necessary- and be miserable if that's what God called for, in exchange for a better and brighter tomorrow.

He knew that it would not be easy to give up the few pleasantries that eased the pain of prison life. He knew from experience that the toughest would be giving up masturbation- the only way heterosexual males could satisfy their primal urges behind the prison walls- but he was determined to breakthrough. The best that prison had to offer- drugs, alcohol, pasta and rice dishes, girly books, and talking on the phone- were no longer even remotely appealing. He wanted his freedom, family, and success- his dreams. And he knew that only God had the keys.

* * *

(U.S.P. Lompoc)

After years of wholehearted submission, devoting his life daily to the Lord, Rob slipped and backslid. He slacked on his studies, prayer and fasting. One day he entertained a sports ticket. "Tickets"- typed menus of the daily sports games that they passed around to book bets on- were popular in prison. Rob checked one out, shrugged his shoulders and thought, "It's just one ticket, no big deal."

One ticket turned into many. He started to regress in other areas of his walk as well. Looking at girly pictures and pornography lead to masturbation, and his bad temper got reignited. He also started getting caught up in various social circles and conflicts that he had previously separated himself from.

Rob truly desired to go home and be the man that his mother had raised him to be. God had shown him that He wanted to use him. That he was meant to be the head of his family and provide strength for them in the areas that they were weak in. And that in Him, Rob could be highly disciplined and devoted, and become a powerful and effective tool for God's will.

Even in his backslidden state, Rob continued to read his Bible, but he noticed that he wasn't receiving the revelation he had grown accustomed to. This lack of spiritual insight moved him to devote even less time to the things of God. He began spending more and more of his time idly playing and watching sports, watching various television shows, etc. He basically fell into the mundane routine of prison life- whatever to make the time go by.

The people who knew Rob and the former seriousness of his walk and relationship with God started to make comments to him about the change they'd observed. They say the truth hurts, and their words cut Rob deeply. Everything that they said was true, and Rob knew it. He was dead wrong. But in his rebellion he turned and lashed out at them. Who were they, anyway, to question, criticize, or voice their opinions about him? He fumed! Their remarks weighed heavily on his heart and mind, though, and he eventually wrote his spiritual mother- Ms. Harvey- and confided in her.

A frivolous sports debate escalated, and an altercation ensued. Rob told the guy that he was arguing with that he didn't want to talk anymore, but the guy would not let it go. They fought and Rob beat the guy up pretty bad. He actually snapped out for a brief moment in rage, but when he came back to who he was he was ashamed of himself.

By actually putting his hands on another man and harming him, Rob realized he had grown further away from God than ever. He could no longer turn a blind eye. The contrast of where he had been to where he found himself was stark, and the words his spiritual mother had sent him in response to his letter flashed before his mind's eye: "God will never leave you nor forsake you. There's a mighty calling on your life to minister and preach His word. It's important that you remain steadfast and get back focused." Rob prayed about it, and God told him to fast.

He made up his mind during that time to get back on point and realign himself back in God's will. He started holding a nightly prayer circle in the cell block again and a Bible study on Sunday afternoons. His church attendance became mandatory, and he started participating more in the services. The gambling, idle time and masturbation all came to a cease. Rob was back! Or, better yet, Christ was back in full affect within Rob.

* * *

(F.C.I. Butner)

Baron and Rob started studying together daily. They would get together either outside or in the recreation building after lunch and go for hours. Their hunger and thirst for God's wisdom and truth was insatiable. Their drive and diligence in seeking God's face and will, coupled with the willing sacrifice of both of their devoted walks, was soon rewarded with powerful revelation.

CHAPTER 2

"PROCESS /PROMISE"

All of God's promises are connected to His processes. The church has focused mostly on God's promises. They have, thereby, inspired a semblance of obedience through incentive-based faith to the detriment of the body. By neglecting to properly focus attention on the processes that accompany God's promises, believers are frequently left confused, and feeling duped and/or misguided when instead of the bliss of blessings and answered prayers they expected they find themselves in more trials and hardships than they began with.

Most people come to the Lord when they are down and out, on their last leg, and/or when no other person can provide them with the answers or help they need. When people find themselves in this state- where nobody, including themselves, can help them- God usually becomes attractive, and they call out to Him. They, in turn, are more receptive to His responses. We see this with the nation of Israel:

> *And the Lord said: "I have surely seen the oppression of my people who are in Egypt, and have heard their cry because of their taskmasters, for I know their sorrows. So I have come down to deliver them out of the hand of*

> *the Egyptians, and to bring them up from that*
> *land to a good and large land, to a land flowing*
> *with milk and honey." (Exodus 3: 7&8)*

God heard their cry, and then came to deliver them to a better place. That better place was their promise- "the promised land." This is His custom dealing with His people. He doesn't force Himself on us, but when we become tired of living without Him and the oppression and pain that usually come as a result of His absence in our lives, and finally call out to him - then He is always there; waiting with open arms- ready to deliver us. Let us now observe what happened to the Israelites after their deliverance:

> *For the children of Israel walked forty years in*
> *the wilderness. All the people who were men of*
> *war, who came out of Egypt, were consumed,*
> *because they did not obey the voice of the Lord*
> *(Joshua 5:6).*

> *They certainly shall not see the land of which*
> *swore to their fathers, nor shall any of those*
> *who rejected me see it. (Numbers 14:23)*

> *The carcasses of you who have complained*
> *against me shall fall in this wilderness, all*
> *of you who were numbered, according to your*
> *entire number, from twenty years old and*
> *above. Except for Caleb, the son of Jephunneh,*
> *and Joshua, the son of Nun, you shall by no*
> *means enter the land which God swore He*
> *would make you dwell in. (Numbers 14:29&30).*

So, why did the Lord give the children of Israel a promise, and then swear that they would not be allowed to enter into it? The answer was where they fell- in the wilderness. So, first, let us question why God delivered them from Egypt but took them into the wilderness in the first place, instead of straight into the Promised Land.

Or why did Abram encounter a famine and have to sojourn in Egypt on the way to receiving his promise? (Genesis 12:10)

Or why did David have to live in caves and face so many trials and tribulations for years after being anointed king before being appointed king? (1 Samuel 1- 2 Samuel 5)

Why did Jesus, the only begotten Son of God, begin His formal ministry until around the age of thirty? (Luke 3:23)

Or, better yet, why was Jesus "led up by the Spirit into the wilderness to be tempted by the devil" before He brought the gospel with the power of God to minister to the people? (Matthew 4:1)

The Process! The answer is the process. The Israelites were delivered from Egypt, but they could not enter the Promised Land unless they passed the test of the wilderness. Their external deliverance (exodus) was out of Egypt and through the Red Sea, but their internal deliverance had to take place in the wilderness. The spiritual chains of captivity and oppression are harder to break than the physical ones, and the psychological ones longer lasting.

The Israelites had been freed from physical Egypt, but remained bound by their customs, culture and mentality (and potentially a host of other spiritual influences). God was therefore unable to establish the promise with that first generation, because they would have simply brought "Egypt" into the Promised Land and defeated His purpose. So, why couldn't God get Egypt out of His people in the wilderness? First of all, they were completely unaware of the internal change and renewal process that was supposed to be taking place. Since the land they were promised was supposed to be "flowing with milk and honey," yet they were stuck in the harsh wilderness, they took their eyes off of God and became blind to His purpose. They started to complain, rebel and actually miss Egypt!

They got totally distracted by their external circumstances, and remained ignorant to the internal work God was trying to do in their hearts and souls. Because they did not truly believe and trust in God to honor His word, they didn't continue to seek Him when His word wasn't established as quickly as they thought it should be. Their affliction was designed to accomplish a purpose, but it never achieved its intended goal because they failed to include God in it.

Attached to every promise of God is a process of God. The process is never enjoyable. It usually feels like a direct contradiction of the promise. This leads many to believe that their dreams or prayers were ignored or unanswered. The Biblical "process" always took place in famine lands, deserts, or in a wilderness. These all represent places of lack, trial and hardship. But remember: your process is purposed to prepare you for your promise!

This principle is prevalent in both nature and society. Childhood, with all of its stages, obstacles and learning lessons, is the human process in preparation for adulthood. Dating (or courtship) is a cultural process designed to afford a couple the opportunity to get to know their potential mate and gradually grow closer before making a more serious commitment.

The public and private schooling system is society's fundamental gauge of aptitude for most professions and fields. It's the respected developmental institution that prepares individuals to succeed and excel in their desired careers or positions of employment. You go through years of schooling to be equipped, then eventually entrusted, with a certain responsibility, task or office, and (generally) the rule is the more education (process) the more money (promise) you will earn.

His love and wisdom in God's role of heavenly Father are made manifest through what feels like hellish circumstances and devilish trials, but are in all actuality His spiritual training grounds. He uses the famine land, the desert, the wilderness, and (yes!) evens the devil to shape, form and prepare you for His promise to be established in your life.

For God to establish the promise apart from the process would be both unwise and unloving, just as it would be for a parent to give the gift of a vehicle to a child without first teaching him/her how to drive. The gift has then become a curse and a probable death trap to the innocent and ignorant child, who only wanted to cruise, though not licensed to do so proficiently and responsibly.

When you received Jesus into your life and heart as both Lord and Savior, you most likely received a "promise" as well. God showed you your own "promised land." It probably consisted of good health, wealth, love and happiness. Whatever were the deepest, purest desires of your heart- these God promised you! He delivered you (at least momentarily) from the chains of your mental and spiritual bondage, and showed you that all things were possible through Him. And you believed! Then, you stepped into the wilderness...this you were neither warned about nor prepared for! Even though it's right there in your Bible- everywhere!

You've been taught (and want to believe) that "in Jesus' name" is some kind of magical phrase that will motivate your genie-God to make everything right. That the pain of the shaping and molding that should take place in your wilderness experience cannot be a part of God's perfect will, and your promise should by all means materialize without delay. The truth is that your entire promise is contingent on your development in the wilderness (i.e. your ability to recognize and cooperate with what He is trying to do on the inside of you).

The good news is that if you have received your promise and you are now in the wilderness, then rest assured you are on your way to your promised land! He is preparing you for the dream that He has already said "Yes!" to! It is literally waiting on you.

The bad news is that if you do not recognize and cooperate with what God is trying to do within you while in the wilderness, you could die right there- having only glimpsed your promise, yet not ever allowed to receive it. The Israelites were just one step away. I wonder how close you are... God said that He is tired of His children dying in the wilderness.

-No More Casualties-

CHAPTER 3

Tish and Baron were friends and brief lovers before his incarceration, but she had stepped up and supported him with her time, money, and love since he'd been down. Their relationship was far from perfect- mainly because his captivity rendered him incapable of being there for her in so many ways. They had broken up and severed ties for some months a couple of years prior, and she'd even bared a son as a result of their separation. Still, through love and with the help of time, they'd been able to reconcile their relationship for the most part, and things were going good for them.

Being six hours away in West Virginia for the past six years had definitely taken its toll on their relationship and played a role in their breakup, so they were both excited about his move to Butner. She was now barely forty five minutes away, and they were anxious to be able to see each other regularly.

The officers who worked the visitation room were stricter and pettier than the ones at Hazelton, but they adapted quickly and made the best of their new situation. They started studying the Bible together again during their visits, and even recommitted to their plans of getting married.

Baron hadn't held his daughter Princess since she was one month old. His relationship with her mother was strained and cordial at best. Since she had neither transportation nor any ties nor relation to Tish, he hadn't seen his daughter the entire time he'd spent in W.V.

Baron believed the biggest blessing of being transferred to Butner would be the location. He was so close to his hometown that he knew that he would get to see at least some of his loved ones often. His family wasn't close-knit, and he hadn't seen anyone but his mother and one of his brothers since he'd been in the feds. However, God had placed key people in his life that seemed to love him unconditionally, and he was truly grateful for them.

Now that he was closer, he planned on making those bonds even stronger and being there to support them in any way that he could- especially spiritually. He'd worked in Workcor the majority of his time to support himself, and that was another blessing- Butner had a Workcor factory.

Workcor were federally run production plants that filled different orders/contracts- primarily for the military. They were basically government-run sweat shops, but they afforded federal inmates the opportunity to make more money than most prison compound jobs offered. Baron was an experienced sewer by that time, and coupled with his gift of gab he made his way into the plant in no time.

He felt like he had it as together as one possibly could under the circumstances. He had a loving fiancé, a great friend in Kat, he was finally close enough to start building a relationship with his daughter, he was self-sufficient, and he'd even been blessed with Rob- a brother and study partner who matched his zeal. Obviously, his biggest impediment remained his imprisonment. What kind of man could be truly happy behind bars? But he could feel it now more than ever- God was about to do something.

Before Baron was designated to Butner, he had asked God to use his transfer as a sign: if he was aligned in His will, allow him to be sent to Butner, but if he wasn't and still needed to see some things to send him somewhere else. He assured God that he would stick with Him and remain faithful regardless, but to grant him that sign. The sign had been received: he was at Butner, so he was indeed in God's will. With a spirit full of expectation, he watched and waited for God's next move.

CHAPTER 4

"THE SECOND BIRTH: BORN AGAIN"

"Most assuredly, I say unto you, unless one is born again, he cannot see the kingdom of God." Nicodemus said to Him, "How can a man be born when he is old? Can he enter a second time into his mother's womb and be born?" Jesus answered, "Most assuredly, I say unto you, unless one is born of water and Spirit, he cannot enter the kingdom of God. That which is born of the flesh is flesh, and that which is born of the Spirit is spirit." (John 3:3-6)

"The process" is pertinent in discipleship as well. A disciple studied under, watched and walked with Jesus for around three years. We have been quick to relate the instructions and promises Jesus gave to His disciples to ourselves, but those disciples were under intense, daily training, and all had close relationships with Jesus. It was to them whom Jesus said, "It has been given to you to know the mysteries of the Kingdom of heaven, but to them it has not been given." (Matthew 13:11)

As relevant to the disciples as graduation is to the student, the healthy growth and progress of Jesus' followers should be marked by spiritual promotion. These "promotions" (or baptisms) in the spiritual realm are seen as "births." The lack of attention paid to the disciple's process, or the disciple's progress, is the primary reason for the lack of growth(underdevelopment) we see in the modern-day saints of today's church. They have not been tutored and matured into the men and women of God that Jesus purposed them to be. They are stopping short and becoming complacent in the baby (seed) or child stages of their calling. While salvation is the single most important step, it is but the first step, or level, of the discipleship process.

You must now eradicate the teaching, notion and mentality that getting saved (your salvation) was or is all that matters. When you accepted Jesus into your life and heart as Lord and Savior, that did not complete anything (unless you happened to pass away the very next moment, then- of course your soul's salvation came right on time!). Rather, it was the start of something. It was a new beginning. You were always meant to grow into something greater. Let us first consider this process in the natural (physical) realm.

A seed is first planted in the earth. There it is nourished with nutrients and water (germinated) until a plant sprouts and eventually breaks the surface. With further growth and cultivation, the plant ultimately bears fruit (or some form of produce with its seed within). Likewise, at the moment of conception, spirit life (seed) is imparted (planted) into the egg (earth). This human embryo is fed and nurtured in the womb, and a baby is eventually born (or the seed breaks the surface) into a new world. This baby evolves through the stages of childhood, adolescence and young adulthood (growth and cultivation) until it reaches its final stage of a fully grown man or woman. These stages are marked by many awkward, uncomfortable and sometimes painful periods of change and development. They are both natural and necessary to complete the human maturation process.

We see, then, in both the plant and human examples, that growth is essential and vital to their ultimate purpose, the cycle of life. If either the plant seed or the human embryo were to get stuck or become stagnate in that beginning stage, or any other stage along the way, most would agree that that would be anomalous, dysfunctional and contrary to their created designs. If not attended to or corrected, that plant or human would either die, need a lot of aid to stay alive, or at best be unproductive in this stunted, underdeveloped state.

This brings us to the spiritual stages of growth and development in Christ. Just as the seed enters the earth and the sperm enters the womb, the life-bearing seed of belief enters the heart of those who receive Jesus. These steps are parallel. The Holy Spirit quickens (or imparts life/germinates) this seed in the heart of the believer, giving life to his/her spirit (which was, just like the ground of the earth, barren before the seed was conceived). This is the first stage, level or phase of the discipleship process. Now you're considered a "Christian," or disciple of Christ.

You have been spiritually birthed, or "born again," as a babe in Christ. You have been "born of the Spirit." Jesus said that you must be born again to "see" the kingdom of God (John 3:3), and this is true. Unless you are born again of the Spirit you can neither recognize nor identify God's kingdom.

The third birth- Jesus goes on to teach- "unless one is born of water and the Spirit, he cannot enter the kingdom of God."(John 3:5) So, we learn here that one must be born once of the Spirit to "see" the kingdom of God, but be born yet again of the water as well to "enter" the kingdom.

This second spiritual birth of the water baptism is equivalent to both the plant coming forth from the ground or the fetus being birthed from the womb. They both go from a dark place into a new world of light and a new stage of development (for the fetus-infancy and for the seed- plant life). Likewise, the water birth/ baptism signifies a level beyond belief- a more dedicated level of commitment to turn from one's old ways and follow Christ as an active member of His body (the church).

This decision "births" the believer into an entirely new level of awareness. This level of awareness is "entering" the kingdom of God, where he now partakes of and displays God's kingdom himself.

The Final Product

Lastly, the believer is matured unto his final stage (the disciple's graduation). This is the birth of produce, or of being able to bear what the Spirit ultimately designed and created you to be able to bring forth. This phase carries the same significance and gravity for the child, plant and baptized born again believer. Without growing and maturing, none of these will be able to produce what they were created to produce. The child will never grow up to be a productive citizen and member of society, the plant will never bare its produce, and the spiritual disciple will never be "as his Master."(Luke 6:40)

If we, as disciples, truly aspire to be as the Master (i.e. Jesus), then we must aspire to live as He lived. This includes doing what He did (producing). The sole purpose of a disciple is to become just like his master, so if his master should leave or pass away it's like he never left or died because both he and his teachings live on through his disciples. This is exactly what happened when Jesus ascended- the apostles (His matured and graduated disciples) continued to teach what He taught and do as He did. First, He produced, and then reproduced Himself in His disciples.

We hear a lot of His teachings being preached, but why is there such an absence of the things He did? For even Jesus proclaimed, "If I do not do the works of my Father, do not believe me; But if I do, though you do not believe me, believe the works."(John lo: 37, 38)

The "works" of a man of God are parallel to the deeds of the productive citizen and the fruit of a full grown plant or tree. The works of the man of God are the evidence that he has been fully matured and molded in the image of Christ to do the will of the Father.

If the will of the Father consisted solely of preaching, teaching and righteous living, then Jesus would not have healed the sick, raised the dead and casted out demons. However, Jesus' ministry was dual- words and works. The Holy Spirit now functions in Jesus' role as Teacher, and it is His job to train (disciple) us to be just like Jesus- to have perfect union with the Father. This is a call to be holy and also to directly oppose what is not (Satan and his kingdom of darkness).

Jesus said, "I must work the works of Him that sent me,"(John 9:4) and, "But the Father who dwells in me does the works."(John 14:10) So, we see then that Jesus' works were the Father's, and they were all contrary to (or in opposition against) the works of the devil. The devil promoted and spread sickness, brokenness and misery. Jesus healed. The devil oppressed through demonic oppression, possession and sin. Jesus set the people free through righteousness, forgiveness and by casting Satan's demons out. The devil's way was death and damnation, while Jesus raised the dead and became the way to salvation.

God's children were never meant to remain "children." The Holy Spirit has revealed that most were never entrusted with the power of God because they never finished maturing, so He could not trust them with it. They never grew up into full grown men and women of God. They got stuck somewhere and stopped short of the ultimate hope of their calling. They learned a lot about Jesus and even learned how to live right, but they never completed the process- they never graduated; and they never learned how to fight.

"Put on the whole armor of God that you may be able to stand against the wiles of the devil," and, "Therefore take up the whole armor of God, that you may be able to withstand in the evil day, and having done all, to stand."(Ephesians 6:11, 13) In these two verses, there are three types of stances mentioned: "stand against," "withstand," and "stand." All three are in OPPOSITION to the kingdom of darkness.

We can simply, "stand," which is choosing to take a stand for God's kingdom by living peaceably and righteously in love. We can "withstand," which entails enduring the hardships and persecutions of the enemy's attacks that come as a result of resisting Satan's influence and rule. But we can also "stand against," which is to counter attack and combat the evil one and his hosts.

CHAPTER 5

Rob had been on the west coast for the past three years, and he was eager to see his family now that he was back in N.C. His mother and his brother came from Gates county- about a five hour drive- to see him for his first visit.

He enjoyed every moment of it, although it was understandably tough when it was time for them to leave. Both inmates and their visitors cherished their time together. When the visits were over it was always sad and sobering for both parties; for the visitors who had to leave their loved ones behind, and for the inmates who had to be left.

Rob had strong family ties, and they were his primary source of support. His Uncle Raymond came to see him the following visit. He lived in Durham- about a twenty minute ride away. He hadn't seen his uncle since 2001, so that was another blessed reunion for Rob. Raymond was active in his church and immediately recognized the "glow" on his nephew, and knew that he had been in the presence of the Lord. They fellowshipped for a couple of hours, but Rob didn't expound too much on the things the Holy Spirit had been teaching him. Rob knew that it wasn't time yet.

Rob intended to get a job with Workcor so that he could provide for himself and maybe even save some money. He was offered an orderly job- cleaning and buffing the floors in his housing unit- within his first couple of weeks at Butner, though, and he accepted it. It wasn't his original plan because he knew that he could make more money working for Workcor, but he had grown accustomed to God's hand and knew that His plan often differed from his own. Rob opted to go with His flow and tried to decipher (discern) what He was up to.

One of Rob's passions was working out, and he dreamed of owning his own gym one day. This was one of his few personal/ secular goals- to complete the necessary correspondence courses to become a licensed personal trainer. He planned to do it through a college in New York that one of his buddies turned him onto.

The one female in his life, a woman named Crystal, was more of a question mark than anything. Since walking with God in this capacity, Rob had had numerous women enter his life then leave abruptly. Like- for no apparent reason; no argument; no explanation- just...gone. Most were women from his past and others he had met through different means (buddies, family, face book, etc.). Either way, he had no clue or idea what caused these different females to leave unexpectedly, but his faith remained rooted firmly in God.

He really didn't understand it, and it hurt at times because he felt like he deserved a woman/companion. Truth be told, he felt like he deserved one more than a lot of his peers at times. Still his faith remained in God. He trusted that God knew what He was doing, and Rob was walking too close with Him to not believe that God was working out his destiny.

Once Rob was informed that he was designated to Butner he began seeking God's face and will for what He wanted him to do there. Rob knew that it was a blessing, but he also perceived that there was a deeper, divine reason and purpose for where he was being sent. He sought God for insight on what that reason and purpose was. He was given one word- "Reformation."

CHAPTER 6

"The Kingdom of God/Heaven"

The first verse in the book of Mark reads, "The beginning of the gospel of Jesus Christ, the Son of God." The fourteenth verse of the first chapter reads, "Now after John was put in prison, Jesus came to Galilee, preaching the gospel of the kingdom of God." So, we see here two "gospels" the gospel of Jesus Christ, and the gospel of the kingdom of God.

Mark was telling the story, or gospel, or "good news" of Jesus Christ, but he makes it clear in 1:14 that Jesus came preaching the gospel, or good news, of the kingdom of God. Jesus is the primary component, or "chief cornerstone," of the gospel of the kingdom- He is the King! But He Himself is not the gospel of the kingdom, just as a kingdom is a "king's domain" not the king himself.

The gospel of Jesus is the good news that Jesus is the Christ (i.e. the Messiah), and that He came to give His life to save all who would believe in Him. The gospel of the kingdom of God is the good news of the King's will for those who inhabit His kingdom.

Jesus said, "The time is fulfilled, and the kingdom of God is at hand. Repent, and believe in the gospel." But which gospel was He referring to? It had to be the one He preached- the gospel of the kingdom of God (which we know cannot exist without/ apart from the gospel of Jesus Christ).

And now when He was asked by the Pharisees when the kingdom of God would come, He answered them and said, "The kingdom of God does not come with observation: nor will they say, 'See here! or 'See there!' For indeed, the kingdom of God is within you." (Luke 17:20&21)

But how can the kingdom of God exist within a person? The Holy Spirit has revealed that the kingdom of God (or the kingdom of heaven) is not only a location with set boundaries and parameters, as in the Almighty's heavenly habitation. Rather, it is also God's government, power and authority established in the hearts and lives of those who believe in the Son, the King.

Likewise, Satan's kingdom is established in the hearts and lives of those who adhere to him and his system (i.e. government) of sin and unrighteousness. Both are unseen dominions reigning within those under their respective control/influence/authority. What you say and do are expressions of what is in your heart. They will identify which king and kingdom you serve.

When Jesus preached, He proclaimed, "The kingdom of God is at hand."(Mark 1:15) He could only say that because He came bearing the words and works of the kingdom of God in full authority and power. Hence, He could announce that the kingdom was "at hand," or right there in their midst- through Him. Jesus was the first ambassador of the kingdom of God; the first representative or official of the highest rank sent from the kingdom of God to the world on a special mission; "the firstborn among many brethren."(Romans 8:29)

That mission was to oppose the kingdom of Satan by freeing those who Satan held bound and oppressed. He then converted them by persuading them to submit their wills and allegiances to the King of kings and Lord of lords. He also was sent to train a crew of disciples to do the same and carry on the mission. What did Jesus do to convince the masses that His kingdom was superior and therefore worthy of their loyalty and devotion? He told and showed the people who were under the influence of Satan's kingdom the better qualities and benefits associated with His own.

These qualities are listed in Galatians 5:22&23 as "Love, joy, peace, longsuffering, kindness, goodness, faithfulness, gentleness, and self-control." The benefits were evidenced through the miraculous healings, the raising of the dead, the supernatural feeding of thousands with only small portions, and the casting out of demonic spirits. Even the miracles of turning water into wine, walking on the sea during a storm, and calming the winds and waves of a storm were signs of His authority and power to transform, provide and protect- all in love. These qualities and benefits were presented in direct contrast to the death, sickness, hunger and pain the people had grown accustomed to while unwittingly subject to Satan's reign in and over their lives.

The kingdom of God is within all who believe in Jesus as Savior, and submit their wills to Him as Lord. The baptism of the Spirit occurs when you believe in Jesus as your Savior; the water baptism should signify your submission to Him as Lord (i.e. the King and Ruler over your life). Being "born again" by the water and Spirit allows you to enter God's kingdom through the inner man (i.e. one's spirit), and access both the qualities and benefits therein (in authority and power- just like the Master and those whom He appointed as apostles).

And as you go, preach, saying, "The kingdom of heaven is at hand."' (Matthew 10:7)

CHAPTER 7

Rob and Baron started getting together every day for Bible study. The only time they didn't was when one of them had a visit. They were individually accustomed to receiving revelation from the Word before they met, but together it seemed that the revelation was much greater. It was as if their collective love and diligence generated a more powerful ability to extract the precious elements and jewels from beneath the surface of the Scriptures.

They began to eat daily from the table of the Lord. "Feast" would actually be a better word. Their studies were never structured or pre-planned. They would simply meet, pray, and then flip to the latest verse or passage that had caught either of their eyes since their last study. At other times, they would just start talking, and the Holy Spirit would lead them to a Scripture. Either way, powerful revelation of God's word was revealed daily. Not most days- everyday! And these weren't the classic, orthodox principles and teachings they'd heard all their lives. What the Holy Spirit was teaching them was dynamic. Amazing! This was "new wine!"(Mark 2:22 and John 2:10)

One day Baron asked, "Man, do you think this is going to KEEP happening?! I mean- every time we get together?"

"Yeah," Rob said confidently and nodded his head assuredly. "It is, EVERYDAY!"

Baron was used to receiving revelation and chewing on it for days, even weeks sometimes. He wondered what would be the Holy Spirit's purpose in unveiling such consistent, new, daily revelations, and where it would take them. There had to be a zenith, he thought. This had to be going somewhere.

Rob, on the other hand, was use to receiving daily insight, but this depth of revelation was a new experience for him. The things that God was showing them were blowing his mind. He didn't quite know what to make of it, and he couldn't see what direction God was taking them either. He comprehended each individual revelation, but couldn't grasp a collective significance. He knew, however, that God was taking them to another level.

In reality, by that time they were both in too deep to back out, anyway. Everything in both of their walks had led up to that point, so regardless of where it took them they were both committed. There would be no looking or turning back. Their minds were made up; their hearts were fixed.

Baron was thirty and Rob was twenty nine. Neither believed they would complete the full-term of their sentences. Both had faith that God would show favor and mercy at some point and reduce the time they'd been given. Still, after federal prison terms under their belts, and at their ages, they knew that they would need God to succeed and make something out of their lives. They were a blessing to each other, but individually they had already placed all of their eggs in one basket- it was God or nothing. No other way held any promise.

They were no longer disillusioned by any street dreams or other illegal ambitions. They were no dummies. One more slip up with the law, and they would both be facing life sentences. God was their last resort, their last realistic shot, and they knew it.

And they planned on taking it. They were all in. They were cordial and greeted the brothers they recognized from the church services when they saw them around the compound, but they hadn't built any personal relationships outside of their own. They met in the recreation building one afternoon and the usual happened- the Holy Spirit unveiled some extraordinary truths.

Greater revelations had led to bigger reactions from the two, although they tried their best to maintain some level of calm and normalcy for the sake of the other men in their midst. This day their excitement was getting the best of them, so they decided to go outside where there would be less people and more space for them to fully react and be themselves.

They relocated to an empty basketball court and continued to expound on their newly found jewels. Their zeal and animation now unbridled, their voices rose as the Holy Spirit continued to fit pieces of an age-old puzzle together in their minds and before their eyes.

They both noticed a tall, large-framed brother they recognized as one of the choir members sit down on the edge of a bench within ear shot. He eventually commented on a Scripture and walked over to the conversation. He was an older brother with a charismatic persona that seemed to share their exuberance over the things of God.

He introduced himself as Alex, and embraced Rob and Baron with a welcome and warm spirit.

CHAPTER 8

"Hebrew 4:12"

For the word of God is living and powerful,
sharper than any two-edged sword, piercing even
to the division of soul and spirit, and of joints and
marrow, and is a discerner of the thoughts and
intents of the heart."(Hebrews 4:12)

The word of God is a weapon of separation and judgment-" the sword of the Spirit."(Ephesians 6:17) In the earthly realm, most look at the word of God as solely the words that God spoke once upon a time to help instruct man in God's ways. Spiritually, though, when the word of God is made manifest it is much, much more.

First of all, we must understand that the word of God becomes alive in our lives when read, spoken, or applied. Every word spoken by the Most High God (YHWH) was, is and always will be full of life, because He is the Creator of life, and all life was created through His word. Whether you believe in God's word or not, His word remains the standard by which all things are upheld.

Everything, action, function, or result that takes place is all intrinsically according to God's Word. As if the living aspect of the Word of God isn't powerful enough, this brings us to "powerful." The Word of God is powerful because with it you can see God's will! Then, you can choose to both either yourself with it and produce blessings, or against it and undoubtedly bring about your demise. God's Word is meant to be the light to your pathway, but it won't force you to make the right or wrong decisions. It will, however, highlight God's will for you based on your decisions.

Before hearing God's word you stumbled through life haphazardly, unaware of the full impact of the choices you made or the "ripple-effect"(series of events) you set in motion by them. The Word of God is powerful because it distinguishes good from evil, and by doing so it forces you to make a conscious decision on which path (and kingdom) you bestow your allegiance.

Finally, the Word of God is "sharper than any two-edged sword." There are many two-edged swords that are extremely sharp, but they are only able to cut through flesh and bone. The word of God is sharper than these because it is designed to penetrate the inner-man.

The Sword's Penetration

The verse goes on to explain that the word of God pierces "even to the division of soul and spirit." Your soul consists of your mind, emotions and will. It is what makes you an individual. It develops your thoughts, feelings and motivations. Your likes, dislikes, and preferences; your soul is made up of all that composes your distinct character and personality. Your spirit is the God given life and energy that animates your soul and body.

The Word of God will separate who you are (i.e. your soul) from the vital life force within you (i.e. your spirit). The purpose of this separation is for His word to penetrate your soul and spirit individually. If your soul has been corrupted by sin and uncleanness, then your spirit has been tainted as well.

God, via His Word, isolates them from each other to regenerate your spirit, and then He can begin the renewal of your soul. This is the proper order of the sword's operation- from the deepest depths of the inner-man on out. The verse then says the sword pierces even unto the division of "joints and marrow." This is in relation to the same "division of soul and spirit."

The sword (the Word of God) is designed to divide and isolate each element of your being- body (joints and marrow), soul and spirit. While you are one "person," the three components that you are composed of each have their own individual natures and require individual attention.

While in darkness, we adhered to the conception that we are all basically weak, possess a singular human nature and that our flaws are too complex and interrelated to ever realistically get a firm grip on them. This is one scheme of the devil's strategy: to encourage us to accept our imperfect conditions by justifying them as simply...human. If we choose to accept our fallen states, while our souls may still remain saved through faith in Christ, we will remain separated from God and ineffective against the enemy.

The truth is that it takes knowledge and discipline to train each aspect of your being (body, soul and spirit) and bring them all into obedience and subjection to Christ. Only by focusing on each element and its weak points can we continue to grow in God. The primary purpose of the word of God is to divide, separate, isolate, then pierce and penetrate these elements with truth and light- forcing you to consciously and knowingly either reject or accept Him.

The final portion of this verse informs us that the Word of God "is a discerner of the thoughts and intents of the heart." The "heart" is a figurative term used to describe the deepest and purest desires of one's inner most man- his spirit. These desires are from God. They are so deep within, though, that in our fallen states they are easily hidden and overshadowed by our soulful desires which are highly influenced by our flesh. Instead of shaping our character from our inner-man (as we were originally designed to do) we- in reverse- allow the fleshly external realm to mold and influence our identities.

This is contrary to our original "human nature" which was created to evolve from the inside out. We now (sadly) allow ourselves to be formed and molded from the outside in. We don't change and impact the world- we're changed and impacted by it. We don't do much acting- we do more reacting.

This current state is a direct result of Adam and "the fall." The word of God highlights the thoughts and intents of our hearts so that we can once again see the things we truly long for- the dreams that God placed in us beyond the surface desires of our minds, emotions and bodies.

The word of God allows us to perceive our true identities in Christ- who God created us to be- and embrace them or remain the selfish, lust-filled, soulful men and women the world has told us we are. On the other hand, if the thoughts and intents of our hearts have become vile and corrupted from too many years of recklessness, lawlessness and sin, the word will illuminate this and encourage us to repent. We see, then, how great and powerful the Word of God really is. It first operates as a sword separating the body, soul and spirit, and then penetrates them with truth. Through this truth, God's Word then functions as a piercing light, exposing the darkness from the light within us, and revealing who we've become and who God created us to be.

This is admittedly complex, but God is now weaning us (the body, the church) off of milk and onto meat (the heavier truths of His word). The Holy Spirit is revealing what the Father simplified for us in Christ like this: And the Word became flesh and dwelt among us. (John 1:14) God sent His Word to us as a Man- Christ Jesus of Nazareth. Jesus, then, proceeded to operate as the "Sword" and separate people.

> *"Do not think I came to bring peace on earth. I did not come to bring peace but a sword. For I have come to 'set a man against his father, a daughter against her mother, and a daughter in-law against her mother-in-law; And a man's enemies will be those of his own household. He who loves father or mother more than me is not worthy of Me. And he who loves son or daughter more than me is not worthy of Me."(Matthew 10:34-37)*

He even separates us from ourselves.

> *"If anyone desires to come after me, let him deny himself." (Luke 9:23)*

He then functioned as the Light. The apostle John wrote about John the Baptist bearing witness to Jesus in this way: "This man came for a witness, to bear witness of the Light that all through him might believe. He was not that Light, but was sent to bear witness of that Light. That was the true Light which gives light to every man coming into the world."(John 1: 7-9) He forced no one to choose Him, but by the Light being made manifest in the flesh, all were forced to see and make a decision nonetheless.

> *"And this is the condemnation, that the light has come into the world, and men loved darkness rather than light, because their deeds were evil. For everyone practicing evil*

hates light and does not come to the light, lest his deeds should be exposed. But he who does the truth comes to the light." (John 3:)

God, in His infinite wisdom, simplified the created purpose and function of His word for all time by sending it in the person of Jesus. When we accept or reject Jesus, we accept or reject His Word in our lives, and either allows it to, or disallows it from being able to, operate therein. Just hearing the gospel of Jesus puts the Word of God to work in hearts and lives: separating, exposing and either imparting life to those who receive it (Him) or condemnation to those who do not.

The Holy Spirit is now unveiling the deeper functions and operations of God's word to further equip us. With this knowledge we can now use this sword with a surgeon's precision, to intentionally and deliberately divide, illuminate, and impart life (or judgment) according to the person and situation at hand. This is not a judgment we "cast." Rather, the word itself is an instrument of judgment that confirms or convicts in the hearts of all who hear it.

The Counterfeit Sword

Satan's M.O. has always been to distort, pervert, and ultimately try to destroy the works (creation) of God. He is not a creator himself, but rather seeks to taint, manipulate and mimic the things in God's creation for his own evil intents. His primary goal is to defile and desecrate the pinnacle of God's creation- man, who was created in God's very image. By doing so, he attempts to mock God and exalt himself as supreme over God before all of creation.

Satan surely recognized the power of God's word from the beginning of this world's creation, and chose to use his own as one of his choice weapons against mankind (e.g. the serpent's deception in the garden of Eden was through Satanic word). While it is weaker than the word of God, it has still proven to be highly effective in its own right. In Satan's attempt to pervert all of God's original creations, his custom has been to piggy-back off of God's original designs, replacing God's noble intents and purposes with his own corrupt ones.

We see this clearly with the counterfeit word of Satan. While God's word (Sword) pierces and penetrates with life leading to life, the devil's pierces and penetrates with darkness leading to death. For instance, God's word will expose a lie and extract it from a relationship, allowing harmony, fellowship and love to abound. The devil's word will infect a harmonious relationship with a lie, producing strife and separation. Even within an individual, God's word(when applied effectively) can pierce and separate the lustful desires of a man's flesh from the faithful and pure intents of his heart, infuse him with the power of God's truth, and lead him to self-control and godliness. On the contrary, Satan's word says that "all men are dogs." So, a man of virtue and self-control can easily be pierced by Satan's sword and persuaded into believing that his desire to be disciplined is unnatural, and that entertaining his fleshly, lustful appetite would actually be more normal or even more "manly." This word is further promulgated through many popular clichés such as, "I'm only human," or, "What do you expect- I'm a man!" These are all part of Satan's arsenal, and seem to be at every man's disposal just waiting to be used and applied as justification. They can lead any man from the pure and righteous guidance of their hearts and spirits and down the path of sexual depravity.

God's Word will always promote life, love and peace. Satan's will always spread strife, confusion and pain. Satan's word is counterfeit no matter how genuine it may appear. It is worthless and can produce no good. It will come in the form of slander, gossip, accusations, conversations that inspire or glorify some sort of lust, vice, greed, or vain and idle babble. It can come cloaked as "good advice," wisdom or even religion. It can pop up in your own mind in your internal dialogue at opportune times.

Receive and feed on the devil's word and you will become confused, weak, and ultimately dismayed and dysfunctional. You will self-destruct, or (more accurately) he will attempt to destroy you with it. Rebuke it and do not entertain it. If you do not consume it, it will not be able to wreak havoc in your life (internally and/or externally). Seek the Word of God- it will make you strong and ultimately victorious. Become skilled in its use and you will fortify yourself, and win territory for God's kingdom in the lives of others.

CHAPTER 9

Baron was housed in the same cell block with the congregation's head usher at Butner- a guy named Vick. Vick observed Baron's walk for a few weeks and presumably approved of it, because he asked Baron if he would be interested in becoming an usher for the church. Baron never elected to involve himself in the church at Hazleton to the extent of holding a formal position, but he always said if he went somewhere he felt the Spirit he would become more active.

He accepted Vick's invitation, and encouraged Rob to join him. Weeks later they were both ushers at Butner. They were walking the track one evening when Alex spotted them. He was walking with a few brothers that Rob and Baron didn't know. Alex greeted them enthusiastically, and then introduced them to the brothers in his company. Alex then asked what Baron and Rob were talking about. They tried to brush him off with some abstract answers, but Alex was relentless. He suggested they gather in a secluded corner to build on the Word.

After praying for the Holy Spirit's presence and guidance, they quoted some Scriptures and began expounding on them. Eventually, the current state of the church as a whole was breached.

"God has been showing us some amazing things about His Word, and how to use it effectively. We've been reading and studying it, but He's shown us that we've yet to use it at its full potential. In Hebrews 4:12, it says that the word is..."

Alex cut him off and completed the line, "sharper than any two-edged sword!"

"Exactly," Baron chimed in.

"And He's shown us that His Word is actually a weapon. An offensive weapon," Rob finished.

"Right, See. . ." Baron started, then held up a hand to pause the exchange as God spoke to his spirit. "The saints for years-generations- they've only defended. Defense only. Nobody's been fighting the enemy back."

"But God is raising up an army," Alex roared, "An army to war against Satan's kingdom!"

There were about five other brothers congregated in a makeshift circle, but they were all somewhat new to the faith. They remained reticent and didn't add much but their smiles, head nods and hand claps. Rob, Baron and Alex dominated the dialogue.

"And to wage war we're going to have to know how to use the sword of the Lord," Rob said. "Jesus defeated the devil in the wilderness with it."

"And He used it to cast out demons," Baron added.

"And to calm and quiet the stormy winds and sea," Alex added.

"And when the troops came to get Jesus they fell to the ground when He said, 'I am He!'" Baron said.

"The Word of God is that powerful, extremely powerful!" Alex recalled.

"Listen," Rob said, and cupped his ear to garner everybody's attention, "we have not been growing to our fullest potential, brothers. And when I say 'we' I'm speaking about the entire body of Christ. The devil has been winning this battle in the lives of believers. He's been doing whatever he wanted to. He hasn't been able to steal their salvation, but he's been a wrecking shop and taking and destroying everything else in their lives."

"And I use to wonder about so many Christians I use to see who believed in Jesus, because they were doing so bad," Baron said, and shook his head regretfully. "I mean, really struggling- like check-to-check and miserable. Now I realize that they were only living defeated lives because they didn't know how to fight! And they didn't know how to fight because no one taught them how!"

"He's about to show us," Rob said confidently, and then looked over at Baron.

"Yeah," Baron agreed and nodded his head as he looked up and over at Rob. "He's about to show us so much."

CHAPTER 10

"RECONCILIATION"

Now all things are of God, who has reconciled us to Himself through Christ Jesus, and has given us the ministry of reconciliation, that is, that God was in Christ reconciling the world to Him, not imputing their trespasses to them, and has committed to us the word of reconciliation. Now then, we are ambassadors for Christ, as though God were pleading through us: we implore you on Christ's behalf, be reconciled to God. (2 Corinthians 5:18-20)

Verse eighteen highlights that God has "reconciled us," or restored and reunited us back into harmony and agreement with Himself through Christ Jesus. He has given us the "ministry of reconciliation," or obligated us to serve others by restoring them to an acceptable spiritual state in Christ.

The catch is at the end of verse twenty, though, which reads, "We implore you on Christ's behalf, be reconciled to God." Paul was writing the church in Corinth. To believers whom, according to verse eighteen, had already been reconciled to God. So, then, why would Paul at the end of verse twenty implore them to be "reconciled" to God? The key is in verse nineteen- "the word of reconciliation."

A "word" from on high, from God, is always deeper than any one thing or meaning. God is so much higher and greater than us that when He sends one word down it is usually multi-faceted with many levels and degrees. He sends it from the supernatural realm encapsulated in one word, and it transforms in the natural into a complex and dynamic series of principles and lessons.

Hence, this 'word of reconciliation' implies that reconciliation to God is another process, and that your initial reconciliation(verse 18) is the beginning of this alignment process that is intended to ultimately bring you into perfect union with God.(verse 20) The different levels of this walk have been firmly established in the 'Process/Promise' and 'Born Again' chapters. Your initial conversion was your first spiritual birth, which reconciled you to God through Christ's blood. The completion of your reconciliation must take place through your continued submission, growth and development (discipleship).

If conversion to faith in Jesus Christ completely reconciled you to God, Paul would have had no need to encourage these believers to "be reconciled" at the end of the passage. It would have been done already. In all actuality, the spirits of the Corinthian believers had been reconciled to God in Christ, but their souls and bodies still needed to be brought in alignment with God's will. Reconciliation had only taken place in part. Being fully reconciled is the hope of our calling.

> *"That they all may be one, as You, Father, are in me, and I in you; that they also may be one in us that the world may believe that you sent me. And the glory which You gave Me I have given to them, that they may be one just as We are one: I*

in them, and You in Me; that they may be made perfect in one, and that the world may know that You have sent Me, and have loved them as You have loved Me." (John 17:21-23)

CHAPTER 11

By the time Baron arrived at the visiting room there was only about thirty minutes remaining in visitation. A female officer who was regularly assigned to the visiting room- Ms. Brown- was known for being mean and hateful to inmates and their visitors.

It seemed like she got some kind of kick out of making their visits unpleasant, and for some reason she seemed to take a special interest in messing with Baron and his visitors. She had rejected both Tish and Kat numerous times for "improper dress-code," which had never happened the previous six years of Baron's incarceration. He got to the visiting room so late that evening because Kat had been turned around yet again, and had to drive to a nearby store to purchase some looser pants and change before Ms. Brown would admit her.

What made the delay even worse, though, was that Kat had brought his daughter Princess. That was the first opportunity he'd had to see her in person since she was an infant. He was nervous, but due to the long delay he was frustrated as well. As he entered the visitation room he tried to calm his nerves. He also sent a quick prayer up, and asked God to rid him of his frustration so that he could enjoy what was left of his visit.

He scanned the room and spotted Kat, and made his way over to where they were seated. Kat had brought her six year old son, too, and Baron spotted him on his way over. He recognized his daughter seated with her back to him. She wore a ponytail, and he could tell it was her from her frizzy hair. A wide grin broke out across Kat's face when she spotted Baron, and she stood and hugged him first. Baron rubbed her son's head and greeted him, then leaned over and embraced his daughter warmly.

Kat immediately began to rave about her frustrations with Ms. Brown, but all Baron could do was stare at Princess. The sight of her amazed him. She was extremely quiet, but Baron hoped that would change in time. He eventually talked her into sitting on his lap. He knew that it was natural for Princess to be aloof and distant because other than talking on the phone from time-to-time, they were strangers. She had been sweet to him over the phone, but she had no recollection of being around him in person, so he understood that she probably felt awkward and uncomfortable.

Baron was a mama's boy, and his mother had raised him with a soft spot for women. Once he began making some real money in the streets, there were different little girls he met in needy situations. He couldn't help but to step up and do what he could to help them out when he could. Before he knew it, he had several illegitimate "little sisters" that he looked out for, and they were all crazy about their "big brother."

These experiences made it seem even more abnormal and almost cruel and surreal for Baron that his own daughter was so uneasy around him. Even after sitting in his lap, Princess would not turn to look him in the face unless he turned her head himself, and she would quickly turn away again. He couldn't imagine his own daughter not falling for him eventually.

CHAPTER 12

"PERFECTION"

> *"... that we may present every man perfect in*
> *Christ Jesus."(Colossians 1:28)*

> *"...that you may be perfect and complete,*
> *lacking nothing."(James 1:4)*

> *"...after you have suffered a while, perfect,*
> *establish, strengthen, and settle you."(1 Peter*
> *5:10)*

> *Therefore, leaving the discussion of the*
> *elementary principles of Christ, let us go on to*
> *perfection. (Hebrews 6:1)*

Ask a Christian if they believe that a man can be perfect. Go
ahead! Ask! Nine out of ten believers will proudly and adamantly
reply, "Of course not! There was only one perfect Man, and that
was Jesus," without even giving the question a second thought.
The Holy Spirit has revealed something radically different and
greater, though- that even Jesus had to be perfected!

> *For it was fitting for Him, for whom are all*
> *things and by whom are all things, in bringing*
> *many sons to glory, to make the captain of*

their salvation perfect through sufferings. (Hebrews 2:10)

Though He was a Son, yet He learned obedience by the things which He suffered. And having been perfected, He became the author of eternal salvation to all who obey Him. (Hebrews 5:8-9)

And if you decide to not believe the writer of the book of Hebrews, Jesus said it Himself. "... And the third day I shall be perfected."(Luke 13:32) One of the primary purposes that Jesus was sent was to clarify and teach us how to think, see, and even act like our heavenly Father- like God! He taught the people that if they did, they would "be perfect" and godly, or more specifically, God's sons and daughters.

"Therefore you shall be perfect, just as your Father in heaven is perfect." (Matthew 5:48)

This led us to look up the word "perfect" in the original language it was written in- Greek. It is derived from the word "teleios" which means "complete or completeness"(i.e. of full age, Man, fulfilled, accomplished, fully matured, perfect).

So we see here that Biblical perfection does not imply without flaw or absence of error as most would assume. Man, in fact, was never designed to never err or make mistakes. On the other hand, it is through man's mistakes that he grows and is matured (trial and error). Hence, the age-old proverb, "Experience is the best teacher."

Man, with God's help, can be perfect. Maybe not flawless but complete. Man can be perfect in Christ despite his/her flaws or shortcomings. He can be completely matured in Christ, equipped for every good work and prepared to properly atone for every failing or misstep. Man can prevail and overcome until he's reached this highly refined and disciplined state of excellence in Christ- perfection. This is the Bible's definition of a perfect man. This is the hope of our calling.

The fall

Although Genesis never states that Adam and Eve were perfect, most Christians have adopted this view based on the fact that they were the first two humans. They were created exactly how God wanted to create man and woman- the prototypical human beings. They were, technically, in a "perfect state" there in the garden, but since they were created as full grown man and woman, they went through no "perfection process." When Eve was deceived into eating the forbidden fruit, Adam partook as a result, and they were kicked out of the garden. Most conclude that this was all a grave mistake.

The Holy Spirit has revealed, however, that this was the beginning of Adam and Eve's perfection process.

A wise man once said that we only truly know what we have experienced. We can memorize all kinds of head knowledge, just like Adam knew not to eat of the forbidden fruit "or else," but we do not truly know what we have learned- whether what we have learned is true or false- until we see for ourselves. This is called experiential knowledge, or wisdom.

The child does not truly know that his/her mother knows best when she tells him/her to not touch the stove until he/she does so and burns his/her hand. A teen does not know that his father's advice is sound when he's instructed to observe the speed-limit until he speeds past it and wrecks his car. Likewise, Adam and Eve did not know that God was good, or that the garden was wonderful, until they experienced the evil intent and deception of the serpent and the hardships they encountered outside of the garden.

When children disobey their loving parent(s) they usually do so to their own detriment. But there are two primary lessons to be learned from the negative consequences of disobedience: (1) to not do what you did again, and (2) that you can trust the advice of your parent(s) because they/he/she has your best interests in mind. And we all know how the story goes- the child does not immediately begin to honor and obey it's parent(s) after the first act of rebellion, but rather continues to rebel throughout the course of childhood and adolescence- living and learning. It was through "the fall" that Adam and Eve learned that their heavenly Father's will for them was all good, and that His commands were indeed in their best interests.

It is, likewise, through our many falls that we eventually learn and recognize that God's will for us was and always is all good, and that His commands are to establish and sustain this goodness in our lives. This is when we begin to submit our wills to Him.

Make no mistake: God makes no mistakes. And He made none with Adam and Eve. He gave them free will, and was well aware of what this free will (which He also created) would produce inside of the earthen vessels He created from scratch in His own image. The Scriptures remind us repeatedly that God knows both the beginning and the end. He cannot be surprised. So it's safe to presume that Adam and Eve's fall was predestined and purposed for mankind's good in God's ultimate plan, and that our individual falls are designed to build and develop us through the tests and trials produced by our bad, ignorant, and rebellious decisions.

Back to Eden

Adam and Eve's fall separated them from God's prosperity (provision) and their intimate relationship (union) with Him. This resulted in hardships, discomfort and ultimately death. They also lost their sensitivity to God's presence in their lives- their ability to walk and talk with Him. When we fall (spiritually) we separate from our Creator as well, and eventually experience the same hardships, discomfort, pain, and death that disconnection with God brings about.

But thanks be to Jesus that we now have the opportunity to attain the state that was lost- to get back to Eden! Through Christ we can realign ourselves in God's will, and become intimately connected to Him, and also experience life in His perfect will and provision. This means restoring our union with the Father, being able to walk with Him, being where He is at, and being involved with what He's doing.

> *And they heard the sound of the Lord God walking in the garden. (Genesis 3:8)*

Also, being able to converse and communicate with Him directly.

> *The Lord God commanded the man, saying... (Genesis 2:16)*

> *Then the Lord God called to Adam and said to him, "Where are you?" So he said, "I heard your voice in the garden. . ." (Genesis 3:9&10)*

This also entails living prosperously and lacking nothing, as our God is God over all things- all resources are at His disposal.

> *Then God blessed them, and God said to them, "Be fruitful and multiply; fill the earth and*

subdue it; have dominion over the fish of the sea, over the birds of the air, and over every living thing that moves on the earth." And God said, "See, l have given you every herb that yields seed which is on the face of all the earth, and every tree whose fruit yields seed; to you it shall be for food."(Genesis l: 28&29)

To attain this state requires being perfected, through our falls, in Christ. What happened to Adam and Eve actually happens with virtually every new life brought into this world. In this light, Adam and Eve were somewhat of a shadow. Every baby is born into a type of "garden of Eden." They are birthed into a new world and are fully provided for and intimately loved. Totally dependent and innocent, who would argue against calling this new born babe perfect (for in the traditional sense, he is without blemish)? No friction exists between this child and its parent(s) until, at some inevitable point, he/she chooses to eat from "the tree of the knowledge of good and evil," or decides to no longer trust blindly and obey but to see for itself if the rules and restrictions placed on him/her are valid and legitimate. Some form of chastisement usually follows.

Some children mature faster than others, but for however long the child remains in this rebellious state they are destined to continue falling- well into adulthood in a lot of cases. Most immature adults are simply legally grown children. All of the falling, however, has the potential to create a well-seasoned and developed character if the mistakes are learned from and one begins to live wisely. The phrase "Adversity builds character," and the old adage, "Only he who travels the deepest depths can attain the highest heights" both recognize this truism.

This "wise living" usually includes some of the advice and/or instructions obtained in a person's upbringing. Many, at this point, confess to their parents that they realize that they always loved them, wanted what was best for them, and were right about almost everything. Practically everyone who is reconciled back to God through Christ makes a similar confession to our heavenly Father. Jesus calls us, when we're sick and tired of falling, back to the childlike state of dependency and obedience Adam and Eve had in Eden. The perfection process can only begin when this child-like state is willfully chosen. The choice is yours to make.

> *"Assuredly, I say to you, unless you are converted and become as little children, you will by no means enter into the kingdom of heaven. Therefore, whoever humbles himself as this little child is the greatest in the kingdom of heaven."(Matthew 18:3-4)*
>
> *"Assuredly, I say to you, whoever does not receive the kingdom of God as a little child will by no means enter it?" (Mark 10:15)*

CHAPTER 13

Rob's unit orderly job only took him a couple of hours every morning to complete. He wished that he could earn a little more money, but he found himself continually ministering to different brother's needs on the rec. yard in the afternoons. This was never his intention, nor did he ever look for anybody. They would seek him out with their concerns and/or issues, and his heart told him to remain content for the time-being. That God was in the midst and to stay put and be patient.

Baron worked in Workcor from 7:30 a.m. to 3:30 p.m. After the visits he received on the weekends and on some weekdays, he and Rob were only left with a few nights a week to get together and build. He wished they could spend more time in God's Word like they use to before he started working, but he had been working and supporting himself the majority of the time he'd been incarcerated. When anybody sent him money he always looked at that as extra. As a thirty year old man, he just believed that he was, and should be, responsible for making his own way-even if he was in prison.

But his writing had also ceased. Baron rapped when he was free on the streets, and he believed then that he was destined to be a rapper. Through God, he came to understand that while he did possess the talent to rap, that didn't mean that rapping was his purpose. His true gift lay in his way with words. He wrote a few books while at Hazleton, and was in negotiations with a publisher who was highly interested in one of his novels. That novel was part one of a planned trilogy, but due to Baron's now crammed schedule he only had sixty pages of the second novel written (and that had been done months prior at Hazleton). He had not written a word since he'd been at Butner.

Rob passed along bits and pieces of personal revelation to Baron in passing, and when they got together they'd expound on them. With the Holy Spirit's help, every revelation- once fully unveiled- was another spiritual explosion in their spirits and minds. It would always gradually come together and coalesce, and they marveled at the impact of each new jewel.

They still had their personal dreams- to be successful, have families, and serve God in powerful ways- but they didn't know exactly how what God was teaching them would play into their destinies. But they could sense that it was going to play some major role. Their teachings were moving in a specific direction.

CHAPTER 14

"ENLIGHTENED EYES"

Paul prayed for the believers in Ephesus, "That the God of our Lord Jesus Christ, the Father of glory, may give to you the spirit of wisdom and revelation in the knowledge of Him; the eyes of your understanding being enlightened; that you may know what is the hope of His calling, what are the riches of the glory of His inheritance in the saints, and what is the exceeding greatness of His power toward us who believe, according to the working of His mighty power which He worked in Christ when raised Him from the dead and seated Him at the right hand in heavenly places. . ."(Ephesians l: 17-20)

Let us first establish that the Apostle Paul moved in all nine gifts of the Spirit, and was blessed with abundant revelation and word from on high that was so ahead of his time the Spirit would not allow him to disclose it all.

> *". . .such a one was caught up to the third heaven. . ."(2 Corinthians 12:2)*

> *"How he was caught up into Paradise and heard inexpressible words, which it is not lawful for man to utter."(2 Corinthians 12:4)*

He had many answers that the Holy Spirit would not allow him to reveal, but he was allowed to leave many clues. Paul prayed that the eyes of the believers would be enlightened. That we would be able to see what he saw and come to know what he knew. There are three things in this passage that Paul prayed believers would come to know: the hope of His calling, the riches of the glory of God's inheritance in us, and the exceeding greatness of His power toward us.

The next piece of this passage provides us with a key to understanding these. They are all "according to the working of His mighty power which He worked in Christ when He raised Him from the dead." This calling, this inheritance, and this power are not in direct relation to Jesus' birth, life, teachings, or even blood sacrifice. These are all according to, or aligned with, Christ's resurrection. This is a "post-death" revelation; when Jesus was raised from the dead a specific door was opened for mankind.

When Jesus was crucified, He paid for our sins with His sinless blood, and made a way for us to be reconnected to God the Father. Through His life, Jesus taught us how to align ourselves in the Father's will and remain in union with Him by joining our thoughts and actions to His own (the Son's). But it is Jesus' resurrection that enables us to embody Him fully as a "joint heir,"(Rom.8:17) as another son of God.

When Jesus was baptized, "the Holy Spirit descended in bodily form like a dove upon Him."(Luke 3:22) This is highly significant because God made a visible show of Jesus receiving the Holy Spirit. It would not have descended on Him if it were already upon or in Him. Rather, this was historic- Jesus was the first Man to access God's own Holy Spirit.

The 'Spirit of God' had come "upon" many men of God in the Scriptures in the span of Israel's history, but never quite like this (or in this capacity). It was never referred to as the "Holy" Spirit in the old testament- only "the Spirit of God or "the Spirit of the Lord"- nor had any man ever done the works that Jesus was empowered to do after receiving this Holy Spirit.

This "Holy" indwelling of God in man was different. It was more powerful and purposeful, for almost anytime the Spirit of God fell on the men of God of old it was for the purpose of establishing God's dominion and kingdom in the physical world through battles and war.

That was only a shadow of God's true intent, though. His intent was to wage war against Satan and gain dominion over the hearts of men. This is the real battleground, for it is through man's allegiance that either God's or Satan's kingdom is actualized on earth through men's lives.

Before Jesus was crucified, He promised His disciples that, "The Helper, The Holy Spirit, whom the Father will send in my name, He will teach you all things." (John 14:26).

> *"It is to your advantage that I go away; for if I do not go away The Helper will not come to you. If I depart I will send Him to you." (John16:7)*

Jesus also taught of the Holy Spirit's functions when He said, "He will glorify me, for He will take of what is mine and declare it to you. All things that the Father has are mine. Therefore I said that he will take of what is mine and declare it to you." (John 14:15)

Jesus was the first Man to have the Holy Spirit dwell within Him. Having accomplished this He died with it, but through His resurrection He kicked the door wide open for all those who believe in Him to be indwelt.

"Most assuredly, I say to you, unless a grain of wheat falls into the ground and dies, it remains alone; but if it dies, it produces much grain." *(John12:24)*

"When He ascended on high, He led captivity captive and gave gifts to men."(Ephesians 4:8)

This same Holy Spirit that empowered Jesus is capable of making us just as He was. This was the hope of His calling for us, the inheritance inside of us, and the exceeding great power toward us Paul prayed we would learn. The original Son of God was sent and revealed over 2,000 years ago. This is the pinnacle of the Holy Spirit's work- to perfect then empower "sons" of God's kingdom.

"Father, glorify your name." Then a voice came from heaven saying, "I have both glorified it and will glorify it again." (John12:28)

The Revealing of the Sons

The Apostle Paul, in Romans chapter eight, was encouraging the believers in Rome to press forward and walk in the power of the Spirit. Evidently, although they were born again believers in Jesus, they did not comprehend what was released to and in them. Therefore, they were walking in the same weakness (the flesh) that they had previously walked in due to their ignorance. Their spirits had been quickened, but since they did not understand the full impact of what had taken place within themselves, they were not cultivating their spirits nor operating at their full potential. They were not accessing or utilizing the power needed (from the Holy Spirit via their spirits) to complete their full transformation. They had stopped short (like today's church). Paul was given complete understanding about what had taken place inside the children of God in Christ, and he was trying to enlighten them through the revelation he'd received.

They were all submissive to their flesh. We were originally created spirit-soul-body, in that order. Our spirits were intended to be our dominant component, filtered to our souls (minds, emotions, and wills), then expressed outwardly through our bodies. As we are now, our bodies (flesh) and souls suppress our spirits and our true Godly spiritual natures. This is our state as a result of "the fall." Through Christ, our spirits have been liberated to dominate our beings again. When we allow ourselves to be led by God's Spirit, we can be fully restored as His sons; God's invisible image reflected in the physical form of man- the pinnacle of His creation.

If not informed about what has taken place in your spirit, although this treasure lies within, you will be incapable of accessing it. Your ignorance will leave you powerless and incomplete. For example, you could be born with the natural ability of an Olympic gymnast, but if never told or trained this talent could lie forever dormant. This is what Paul feared- that those whom God had called in Christ would never taste the power of full redemption and restoration as he had.

"For the earnest expectation of the creation eagerly waits for the revealing of the sons of God." (Romans 8:19)

The entire creation (i.e. mankind) is waiting for the children of God to step up and claim their "sonship."Every human being has lived with the growing gut feeling that we are supposed to be greater than what we are. An intrinsic pulse moves us to believe there is unlocked power and potential within ourselves. The whole creation is waiting on us to complete what we began; to fulfill the hope of our calling; to finish.

> *"For the creation was subjected to futility, not*
> *willingly, but because of Him who subjected it*
> *in hope." (Romans 8:20)*

Mankind has been subjected to futility in that ever since "the fall" we have been manipulated and primarily controlled by our flesh. This has led us to seek fulfillment in fleeting passions, lusts, and countless temporal goals. This is all vanity, or grasping for the wind, as no fleshly desire can ever be fully quenched or satisfied. Also, no mental or material goal can fulfill a man's purpose. God subjected man to this futile state in the hope that man would "come to" one day, seek his Creator for guidance, and be led back to his original purposed state (where his spirit is connected to God and is the primary source of his will).

> *"The creation itself will be delivered from the*
> *bondage of corruption into the glorious liberty*
> *of the children of God." (Romans 8:21)*

Ultimately, the entire creation of mankind will exist in this spirit-led, liberated state. This is and always was God's original plan, and it will be fulfilled. Man will not remain in this current fallen state. However, whether they know it or not, mankind is earnestly waiting on the sons of God to lead the way out of corruption to liberty.

> *"For we know that the whole creation groans*
> *and labors with birth pangs." (Roman 8:22)*

Paul wrote that "we know"- the children of God know how it feels to grope for something more out of ourselves, because we were once a part of "the creation," or the rest of mankind. The Spirit of God acts like a midwife, coaching us and aiding the birth of what's in our spirits until it's manifested outwardly or revealed. Only by walking, or being led, by the Spirit can that which God impregnated in us be developed through the stages of spiritual pregnancy and come forth. Paul goes on to write that they have been laboring and groaning "until now." This is because he believed that it was time, even way back then, for God's children to step up, walk according to the Spirit and be revealed in power (i.e. as he was).

Throughout this chapter (Romans 8), Paul frequently uses the terms "we" and "us" in reference to the body of believers that he is addressing. He includes himself, even though he is the one teaching; in an effort to not exalt himself or appear to have obtained something that they could not. In actuality, Paul had indeed attained this liberated, glorious state- evidenced by his fruits.

> *"Now God worked unusual miracles by the hands of Paul, so that even handkerchiefs or aprons were brought from his body to the sick, and the diseases left them and the evil spirits went out of them." (Acts 14: 11, 12)*

He was far from satisfied with his sole redemption and restoration, though. He yearned for the rest of the body of Christ (the church) to be magnified as well.

> *"Not only that, but we also who have the first fruits of the Spirit, even we ourselves groan ourselves, eagerly waiting for adoption, the redemption of our body." (Romans 8:23)*

When Paul referenced those who had the "first fruits of the Spirit" he was writing about the apostles and anyone else at that time who had reached their full spiritual potential in Christ. He noted that these groaned within themselves, waiting for "the redemption of our body." Notice- he doesn't write "our bodies" but "our body." This is because spiritually matured men and women of God view "the body of Christ" as their own body! Magnified in union with Christ, His corporate body becomes their own; an extension and reflection of themselves; the fruit of their work and ministries. This is why Paul was not at peace with his personal spiritual accomplishment. The evidence of His faithfulness and effectiveness were the souls God had entrusted to him.

In this we see that Jesus' greatest works were not the things He did for man, but rather His ability to reproduce Himself in man. This was the pinnacle of His teachings, miracles, and earthly ministry. The graduation of his disciples to apostles was the completion of the "work" the Father gave Him to do. (John 5:17) Restored, redeemed, trained in spiritual warfare and rooted in love- they were now perfected like their master! They had become sons of God, and He prayed for them this way.

"I have glorified You on the earth. I have finished the work which You have given Me to do. And now, O Father, glorify Me together with yourself, with the glory which I had with You before the world was. I have manifested Your name to the men whom You have given Me out of the world. They were Yours, You gave them to Me, and they have kept Your word. Now they have known that all things which You have given Me are from You. For I have given to them the words which You have given to Me; and they have received them, and have known surely that I came from You. They have believed that You sent me. I pray for them. I do not pray for the world but for those whom You have given Me, for they are Yours. All mine are Yours, and Yours are mine, and I am glorified in them. Now I am no longer in the world, but

these are in the world, and I come to You. Holy Father, keep through Your name these whom You have given me that they may be one as we are. While I was with them in the world, I kept them in Your name. Those whom you gave Me I have kept; and none of them is lost except the son of perdition, that the scripture might be fulfilled." (John17: 4-12)

CHAPTER 15

Baron entered the rec. building and scanned through the sea of inmates looking for Rob's dark-skinned, bald head and low cut beard. He spotted him quickly sitting at a table at the rear of the room. He approached and took a seat across from him.

"What's up, bro?"

"What's up? How was your visit yesterday?" Rob inquired.

"Ah, man, it was a blessing. Tish came up. Man, I love that girl."

Rob nodded his head in approval. "That's good. So, what are you going to do?"

"What do you mean?"

"Man, you know what I mean! What are you going to do with Tish?"

"I ain't gonna lie, man, I want to marry her. Scared, though, you know? Being in this situation; anything can happen."

"Yeah, I know what you mean," Rob said understandingly.

Baron truly loved Tish, but after their breakup and the baby boy she'd had as a result of it, he didn't know if he could ever trust her fully again. From a carnal, worldly perspective he had nothing to lose. Most inmates would jump at the opportunity to "lock in" a good woman for the duration of their stints just to have a little stability and support. Baron had vowed years ago to never play games with a woman again, though, and he wasn't the type to invest his time and mind into something he didn't believe in.

His mother raised him with old-school values, and he'd always said that he was only going to get married once. He wasn't sure if Tish was worth the risk under the circumstances, or if it was even fair to her (even though she'd elected to be faithful) to hold her to that standard and those expectations under the conditions. He also questioned whether she had truly made a mistake (as she claimed) when she left him and slept with her ex, or if he'd been allowed to glimpse who she truly was.

Baron said, "I do have a confession to make," then looked away and smirked. Rob peered at him but waited patiently. "Man, God has been convicting me in visitation about lusting over her so much. I'm talking about; I'm crazy about this girl! And with her sitting in front of me for hours looking all good just. . ." Baron said, smirked again, then dropped his head and ran a hand over his dreads.

Rob smirked himself. He could definitely sympathize with Baron's plight, but didn't really know what advice to give him. They were already incarcerated and deprived of being able to have sexual relations with women, so it wasn't like his brother was fornicating. Still, he was confessing that his lust was getting the best of him. Rob didn't know where to draw the line. He decided to just listen and not cast judgment. He couldn't imagine telling his brother not to desire a woman whom he loved dearly, and who had been there for him for so many years.

Baron continued, "I mean, being realistic, if I'm going to marry a woman and never deal with another, then I need to be crazy about her. So, if God blessed me with Tish, and she does have everything that I want in a woman, then it makes sense that I can't be around her for long without her driving me crazy. I mean, He knows what it's gonna take to sit me down and make me do right by a woman. Still, I can't help that I feel convicted for sitting in front of this woman and lusting over her for hours. But, then, if she didn't turn me on like that there's no way I would even consider marrying her! I'm stuck!"

"I don't know what to tell you, bruh. What did God tell you about her?"

"I don't know. I haven't really asked Him directly."

"Well, that brings me to the next topic at hand."

"What's that?"

"God told me that we need to fast," Rob informed him.

"That's cool. I'm with that. When?"

"This weekend, the next 72 hours."

"No food? No water?"

"No food, no water- Friday to Sunday."

"Let's go."

CHAPTER 16

"BIND AND LOOSE"

The physical ailments and mental disorders that plague mankind are all rooted in the spirit realm. The medical and psychological fields would have us believe that these unhealthy, dysfunctional and painful states are the results of genetic defects, chemical imbalances in the brain or weak immune systems. However, Jesus healed the multitudes with no degrees of higher education.

> *And the Jews marveled, saying, "How does this Man know letters, having never studied?"*
> *(John 7:15)*

Jesus had no PhD in medicine or psychology. His focus was solely on the spiritual condition of those who had need "of the physician."(Mark 2:17) When Jesus ministered to the sick He identified and diagnosed their conditions, just like any other doctor would, but He did this according to their spirits. The deepest that brain scans, X-rays and other modern techniques and findings can delve into is the mind and body. The problem with this is that the mind and body actually show the effects (or evidence the condition) of an individual's spiritual state. Allowing our collective attention (the national and global status quo) to be diverted away from the spirit has been a grave and costly error on our part; an extremely effective, virtually undetected strategy of the evil one.

Before we continue, let us be clear: the mastery(or at least the full comprehension) of everything unveiled by the Holy Spirit up to this point is absolutely necessary for you to ever experience the reality of this teaching in full.

Your personal "process" is paramount. You have to be occupied by the Holy Spirit, and Jesus (through the Holy Spirit) must be your literal Lord, for you to ever be entrusted with these keys. If you attempt to authorize yourself by simply choosing to use these terms and techniques they will possess no power, and you risk shaming yourself and the kingdom you are claiming to represent. Your intentions may be good, but please do not allow your zeal to misguide you into thinking that you can wield the power and authority of God at your own will. He only gives His power and authority to men who have submitted to His will.

You cannot TAKE the keys of the kingdom- they must be given to you. We are giving the knowledge of these keys to the church to help birth those whom God has prepared to enter this next dimension in Christ, and to inspire those whom have not fully submitted to God with what awaits them. Either way, you cannot skip any grades. You must pass each one of them until you graduate. He will give you the green light when you are ready. Until then, you must be patient and grow.

> *"And I will give you the keys to the kingdom of heaven, and whatever you bind on earth will be bound in heaven, and whatever you loose on earth will be loosed in heaven." (Matthew 16:19)*

Once you are sanctioned (or enabled) to enter the kingdom of God (through the spirit and water births) you should inevitably reach this plateau- if you continue to progress. Notice- Jesus told Peter in the above verse "I will give you" vs. "I am giving you," implying that Peter had not yet reached this stage but was in route. Once you've reached this level, you have reached an access point of greatest importance.

We (mankind) lost the majority of our spiritual consciousness (awareness), as well as our positions of power and authority, as a result of "the fall." Jesus came to restore us (our consciousness, power, and authority), and was making known to Peter that when he received the keys to the kingdom he would be restored to a position where he could bind and loose in the natural and spiritual. So, why must a thing be bound and loosed in heaven and on earth?

What is happening when something is being bound or loosed in heaven? The Holy Spirit revealed this: the ability to bind something, or grab and hold something within your grasp, requires some degree of strength. Specifically, you must possess more strength than whatever it is you intend to bind. Jesus used this method (or weapon) to exercise His power and authority over the forces He opposed. He then loosed the people these forces (sin and unclean spirits) held bound.

With these keys, Peter's word would be as the Master's- backed by the power and authority of the Throne. Peter would be authorized with and by the authority of heaven itself to remove sin, command the unclean spirits and liberate God`s children. This authorization and graduation is one of the expectations of our calling.

Binding and Casting

Before Jesus healed the multitudes, He had to have some recognition of faith. Faith is essential to access the power of God.

God does not attempt to inspire faith; He's inspired by it. He is neither moved nor motivated by the faithless. He shows up and shows out for the faithful.

> *"Now He did not do many mighty works there because of their unbelief." (Matthew 13:58)*

> *"Do not be afraid; only believe, and she will be made well." (Luke 8:50)*

> *"Did I not say to you that if you would believe you would see the glory of God?" (John 11:40)*

Next, He would proceed to discern, and then address, one of two spiritually bound states: sin (personal or inherited) and/or demonic oppression.

> *"But that you may know that the Son of man has power on earth to forgive sins" -He said to the paralytic, "I say to you, arise, take up your bed, and go to your house." (Mark 2: 10&11)*

We see here that after the sin was forgiven (which restored the man's spiritual state to perfection) then the healing took place as a result.

> *"See you have been made well. Sin no more, lest a worse thing come upon you." (John 5: 48)*

Jesus made a direct correlation between the crippled man's condition and sin.

> *And when they had come to the multitude, a man came to Him, kneeling down to Him and saying, "Lord have mercy on my son, for he is epileptic and suffers severely. For he often*

falls into the fire and often into the water."
(Matthew 17: 14, 15)

"And Jesus rebuked the demon, and it came out
of him; and the child was cured from that very
hour." (Matthew 17: 18)

From the following passage, we see an effort to try to explain/
diagnose the son's condition as a physical disorder (epilepsy)
in some translations, and as a mental one (lunacy) in the King
James Version. Jesus identified it as a demon.

And when he stepped out on the land, there
met Him a certain man from the city who had
demons for a long time. And he wore no clothes,
nor did he live in a house but in the tombs. And
when he saw Jesus, he cried out, fell down
before Him, and with a loud voice said, "What
have I to do with you, Jesus, Son of the Most
High God? I beg you, do not torment me!" He
had commanded the unclean spirit to come out
of the man. For it had often seized him, and
he was kept under guard, bound with chains
and shackles; and he broke the bonds and was
driven by the demon into the wilderness. Jesus
asked him, saying, "What is your name?" He
said, "Legion", because many demons had
entered him. (Luke 8: 27-30)

In this day and age, a man with such a condition would be quickly
classified as having some form of mental disorder; maybe a
severe case of schizophrenia. He would most likely be heavily
medicated and sedated and put away in some kind of psyche-
ward. Unbeknown to the highly educated psychiatrists and

psychologists, this man would continue to suffer from demon possession.

Once Jesus established the necessary faith and identified the source of the problem, He could then bind and cast it away from the sick or affected individual(s). To bind something in the spiritual realm requires spiritual power.

> *"Or how can one enter strong man's house and plunder his goods, unless he first binds the strong man? Then he will plunder his house." (Matthew 12: 29)*

> *"When an unclean spirit goes out of a man, he goes through dry places, seeking rest, and finds none. Then he says, 'I will return to my house from which I came.'"(Matthew 12: 43, 44)*

These two verses in Matthew chapter twelve shed light on each other. First of all, Jesus spoke of a "strong man" in verse twenty-nine. He identified the strong man as an "unclean spirit" in verse forty-three. For Him to describe the unclean spirit as strong coincides with His teaching that "one stronger than he" must come upon the spirit to overtake it. (Luke 11: 22) The "house" referenced in verse twenty-nine is identified in verses forty-three and forty-four as a "man". So, we see then that we- as men- are "houses" that the spiritual realm is vying for possession of/ ownership over.

Jesus was sent to take back what the devil had stolen (the residency of the house; the power over men), and to teach His disciples how to do the same. First, He would bind the sin and/ or unclean spirits, then remove them from the person (house, premises, vessel). This wasn't always depicted verbatim, but the Scriptures provide ample evidence.

"For which is easier to say, and 'Your sins are forgiven you,' or to say, 'Arise and walk?'" *(Matthew 9: 5)*

Jesus forgave the sin which uprooted and removed it, and then the healing was evident.

When evening had come, they brought to Him many who were demon-possessed. And he cast out the spirits with a word, and healed all who were sick. (Matthew 8: 16)

This is one clear passage depicting Jesus casting out unclean spirits before He could heal the sick. Sin and demons "bind" people, or hold them under spiritual bonds of oppression and control. Sometimes it's sin or demons, and sometimes it's a combination of both. The effects of this bondage are evidenced in physical ailments and/or mental disorders (ranging from mild to severe conditions based on the depth of the sin or the severity of the demonic attack). People are earthen vessels that house spirits and souls, and it is when these are bound internally that the effects are manifested externally through various conditions. A man who is totally free and healthy spiritually should have no physical or mental defects or deficiencies because one's spirit is the source of one's mental, emotional and physical well-being. Jesus came to redeem and restore us, and to use us to bring redemption and restoration to others.

Loosed

And behold, there was a woman who had a spirit of infirmity eighteen years, and was bent over and could in no way raise herself up. But when Jesus saw her, He called her to Him and said to her, "Woman, you are loosed from your infirmity." (Matthew 13: 11, 12)

"So ought not this woman, being a daughter of Abraham, whom Satan has bound- think of it- for eighteen years, be loosed from this bond on the Sabbath?" (Matthew 13: 16)

Immediately his ears were opened and the impediment of his tongue was loosed, and he spoke plainly.(Mark 7: 35)

And He said to him, "Go wash in the pool of Siloam" (which is translated Sent). So he went and washed and came back seeing. (John 9: 7)

Then they came to Jesus, and saw the one who had been demon-possessed and had legion, sitting and clothed and in his right mind. And they were afraid. (Mark 5: 15)

He answered and said, "Whether He is a sinner or not I do not know. One thing I know: that though I was blind, now I see." (John 9: 25)

And certain women, who had been healed of evil spirits and infirmities- Mary called Magdalene, out of whom had come seven demons, and Joanna, the wife of Chuza, Herod's steward, and Susanna, and many others...... (Luke 8: 2, 3)

CHAPTER 17

For Rob, fasting had always been a way for him to draw closer to God. It had become an important part of his spiritual walk. God showed him that it was needed to help bring his flesh into subjection to his inner man- where Christ dwelled. The more he fasted the more it felt like a requirement. Through fasting his prayer life became stronger. Also his knowledge and understanding of the word got deeper.

Baron had only fasted a few times over the span of his walk. From what he gleaned from the Scriptures, it was mainly a tool used by man to move God's heart (he would later come to understand it didn't move God's heart-it connected you to it). The last time he used the "Ester fast" (the one she used in the Bible book Ester) as a model (seventy-two hours; no food- no water) were the three days leading up to his sentencing... when instead of the miracle he'd prayed for and fasted for- he'd received a lengthy prison sentence. It discouraged him from fasting altogether. He had done less intense fasts since then, but it wasn't a regular part of his walk. When Rob brought it up he was ready because he felt it was an area he was lacking in yet fully capable of embracing.

Rob and Baron got together before the fast to write out their petitions and spiritual battle plan. They were excited to put some of the kingdom teaching and spiritual weaponry that they had recently learned about to use. They planned on operating in two offices during the fast: "High Priest"- which would enable them to approach God's throne (through Jesus blood) to intercede and present their petitions, and "Warrior/Soldier"- to fight (in the spirit) against the enemy and his opposition. Their petitions included their secular dreams, insight concerning the women in their lives, their families, their freedom, and their relationships with the Father.

After "writing the vision plainly" (Habakkuk 2: 2) they were both pumped up about the fast. They both had spirits of expectancy, and they believed deeply that God was going to move. They didn't know how or in what capacity; they didn't want to tie God's hands in any way. They definitely believed their breakthrough was on the way.

CHAPTER 18

"CONDUITS"

Then they brought to Him one who was deaf and had an impediment in his speech, and they begged Him to put His hand on him. And He took him aside from the multitude, and put His fingers in his ears, and He spat and touched his tongue. Then, looking up to heaven, He sighed, and said to him, "Ephphatha,"that is, "Be opened." Immediately his ears were opened, and the impediment of his tongue was loosed, and he spoke plainly. (Mark 7:32-35)

Then He came to Bethsaida; and they brought a blind man to Him, and begged Him to touch him.

So He took the blind man by the hand and led him out of the town. And when He had spit on his eyes and put His hands on him, He asked him if he saw anything. (Mark 8:22, 23)

They begged Jesus to "put His hand on" and "touch" both of these men, and He used His own spit to heal both of their conditions. But why did He have to touch them and use spit? Why couldn't He just speak their healing as He did at other times?

> *The centurion answered and said, "Lord, I am not worthy that you should come under my roof. But only speak a word, and my servant will be healed."(Matthew 8:8)*

> *Then Jesus said to the centurion, "Go your way, and as you have believed, so let it be done for you." (Matthew 8:13)*

Or why could't they simply touch the hem of His garment?

> *And when the men of that place recognized Him, they sent out into that entire surrounding region, brought to Him all who were sick, and begged Him that they might only touch the hem of His garment. And as many as touched it was made perfectly well. (Matthew 14:35&36)*

Or why didn't He anoint everybody with clay and give them instructions? Or, once again, just touch everybody?

> *When He had said these things, He spat on the ground and made clay with the saliva; and He anointed the eyes of the blind man with the clay. And He said to him, "Go, wash in the pool of Siloam" (which is translated, Sent). So, he went and washed, and came back seeing. (John 9:6&7)*

> *Now when Jesus had come into Peter's house, He saw his wife's mother lying sick with a fever. So He touched her hand, and the fever left her. (Matthew 8:14&15)*

The Holy Spirit has revealed the purpose of Jesus' various methods: conduits. There exists a "gulf," or bridge of separation (i.e. divide), between the physical and spiritual realms. From the Bible, we know about the existence of God, the devil, and various angelic spiritual entities, but we do not all co-exist in the same dimension (or reality). We (humans) exist in the physical/material realm, and they in an unseen, undetectable spirit realm. Spiritual power must be accessed through some conduit or channel to transfer from the spirit world to our own. It seems that nothing from either side can breach the other at will or whim (of course, with the exception of God the Creator of all realms, worlds and realities).

The source of our electricity is a nearby power plant. Electrical power is generated there, and then distributed to homes, businesses and other establishments through electrical wires. These wires contain copper, which is the standard metallic conduit we use to transfer electricity effectively from point A to point B. This same principle applies when transmitting power from the spirit realm to the physical.

Life existed in the "supernatural"(spirit) before it ever did in the natural. The Bible is clear that everything came from God, and that He is Spirit (John 4:24). So, that realm existed first, and it is the power source of this realm. The Spirit is the source of all energy and life.

We have already established that the source of mankind's ills and disorders are spiritual (i.e. within his/her spirit; a result of his/her spiritual state). Jesus did not superficially band-aid and medicate the effects of people's ailments (mental or physical). He uprooted their source from people's spirits. To do so took spiritual power. He not only had to have the authority to access it, He had to have the means by which to transfer it from the spirit realm (point 'A') to the physical man (point 'B').

The purest conduits from the spiritual to the physical are unseen. They are love (compassion), faith (evidenced by works), and the Word of God. Every time Jesus healed or performed a miracle via His word, these components were all at play. The power of His love, combined with the power of an individual's faith, allowed the power of God to bypass all physical conduits and be transferred through Jesus' word alone. We will expound on these powerful spiritual conduits (or "keys") later in the book. Let us now focus on the more tangible ones.

The size of an electrical wire determines how much electricity can be channeled through it. Different devices require different amounts of power to function. Once the wire is plugged into the socket, the necessary amount of electricity can be accessed and transferred to the device. If the wire is not big enough to carry the proper amount of power to the device,the device will not operate -if too much power is distributed to it, it can blow up or burn out. It's not "one size fits all." The wire, or electrical conduit, must be designed to receive and distribute the proper measure of power according to the device.

In the same way, the man of God serves as the primary conductor (i.e. the human socket) for the power of God, and any other conduits that he may need to use to get the power through to an individual are like increasing the size of the wire for more power output. The primary way God manifests His power to man on the physical plane is through another man (i.e. the earthen vessel). To access this power takes breaking through to the spiritual realm, or connecting to a man of God. You must either become the conduit yourself, or find a man who is one and connect to him. Either way, someone has to be plugged in to the power source, and the one in need has to believe both in God and in His man.

The size of the electrical wire is parallel to the means required- to get the power of God through. How much the man of God must do to get the power through is dependent on the degree of faith the one in need possesses. The more faith that he possesses, the less the man of God must do to get the power through; the less faith, the more he must do.

The Holy Spirit has highlighted five levels of faith that people possess. The less faith that the person in need had the more conduits Jesus had to use to produce the healing. The more faith the individual(s) possessed, the easier it was for Jesus to channel the supernatural power they needed through. We'll repeat five verses that were quoted at the beginning of the chapter, now in order, to identify the five levels of faith Jesus ministered according to.

Five Levels of Faith

1st Level: Very Small Faith.

The man in John chapter nine had been blind since birth. He had to have some measure of faith for Jesus to be able to minister to his condition, but it was very small. This was evidenced by the amount of conduits Jesus had to use to manifest God's power.

> *When he had said these things, He spat on the ground and made clay with the saliva; and He anointed the eyes of the blind man with clay. And He said to him, "Go, wash in the pool of Siloam" (which is translated, Sent). So he went and washed, and came back seeing. (John 9:6&7)*

Jesus was the primary conductor, and He used His (1) spit, (2)the earth(to make the clay), He (3) touched him when He anointed his eyes with clay, the (4)Word of God was spoken when He gave the man instructions, and He needed (5) the water from the pool He told the man to wash in.

2nd Level: Small Faith

The deaf and speech impaired man in Mark chapter seven only had a little more faith than the first level.

This was evidenced by the absence of two conduits Jesus had to use in the previous case.

> *Then they brought to Him one who was deaf and had an impediment in his speech, and they begged Him to put His hand on him. And He took him aside from the multitude, and put His fingers in his ears, and He spat and touched his tongue. Then, looking up to heaven, He sighed, and said to him, "Ephphatha," that is, "Be opened." Immediately his ears were opened, and the impediment of his tongue was loosed, and he spoke plainly. (Mark 7:32-35)*

Jesus used His (1) touch, (2) spit, and (3) word to open the man's ears and loose his tongue.

3rd Level: Moderate Faith

Peter's wife's mother surely knew who Jesus was, and had certainly heard the reports of the miracles that had been done by Him. She might have witnessed His power, or the evidence of it, first hand. Jesus had to do no more than touch her to fully revive her.

> *Now when Jesus had come to Peter's house, He saw his wife's mother lying sick with a fever. So He touched her hand, and the fever left her. And she arose and served them. (Matthew 8:14&15)*

4th Level: Strong Faith

The woman who suffered from a "flow of blood" believed so much that she did not even have to speak to Jesus nor touch His body, but needed only touch the hem of His garment to be made well.

> *Now a woman, having a flow of blood for twelve years, who had spent all her livelihood on physicians and could not be healed by any, came from behind and touched the border of His garment. And immediately her flow of blood stopped. And Jesus said, "Who touched me?" When all denied it, Peter and those with him said, "Master, the multitudes throng and press You, and You say, 'Who touched Me?' But Jesus said, "Somebody touched Me, for I perceived power going out from me." Now when the woman saw that she was not hidden, she came trembling; and falling down before Him, she declared to Him in the presence of all the people the reason she had touched Him and how she was healed immediately. And He said to her, "Daughter, be of good cheer; your faith has made you well. Go in peace."(Luke 8:43-48)*

And then, based on her faith and testimony, a whole region of strong faith!

> *And when the men of that place recognized Him, they sent out into all that surrounding region, brought to Him all who were sick, and begged Him that they might only touch the hem of His garment. As many as touched it was made perfectly well. (Matthew 13:35&36)*

5th Level: Great Faith

> *The centurion answered and said, "Lord, I am not worthy that you should come under my roof. But only speak a word, and my servant will be healed." Then Jesus said to the centurion, "Go your way; and as you have believed, so let it be done for you." (Matthew 8:8&13)*

This was the greatest caliber of faith Jesus encountered during His earthly ministry. With faith this great, Jesus did not even have to be present with the afflicted person for the healing to take place. All He had to do was speak a word to transmit the power.

Focusing on all of these secondary conduits and methods, let us shift back to the primary one: the graduated disciple, the sent man of God; God's earthly conductor. Jesus was the fully accomplished, zenith prototype human conduit used to channel God's supernatural power from the heavens to the earth, and the apostles were our examples of this prototype reproduced. Even before Jesus, whomever the "man of God" in Israel was at any given time was the willing earthen vessel God used to manifest Himself and His power before the people. Nobody embodied this function more completely, selflessly, and as effectively as Jesus Christ of Nazareth, though.

He is the Author and Finisher- our Blueprint- our Forerunner and our Master key. To become a perfected man of God, a refined golden vessel for the kingdom- able to be used as a primary conduit and conductor for God's power to channel through to a sick and needy world- is a huge part of the hope of our calling.

CHAPTER 19

This fast was tougher for Baron than previous ones, mainly because of all of the movement. In the past when Baron would fast, he would usually minimize his movement to preserve his energy. He wouldn't go outside or walk around too much. He'd just do a lot of praying and resting. This was his first time fasting with a partner, though, and because of their plan to pray over their petitions together and fight in the Spirit, he and Rob met frequently on the yard and in the recreation building.

At Butner, each housing unit consisted of two big cell blocks, one sitting on top of another. Baron's cell was on the second floor of an upper cell block; that put him four stories up. So every time he met with Rob it was four flights down and back up. The traveling had taken its toll by day two, and by day three his energy was completely zapped. Still, he continued to meet with Rob and stick to the battle plan.

Their battle plan was the only difference for Rob. Day one had always been fairly easy for him, and day two was usually the roughest. This time he caught a cold on day two as well, though, which added an extra element of challenge and trial. It had happened once before, and he pondered over its significance. It wasn't like he was going to break his fast, but it seemed like some kind of cruel, added attack and he wondered what for. He stayed the course, however, because he definitely wanted to receive whatever God had for him.

God answered all of their petitions and questions in one way or another. They spent a lot of time studying scriptures that pertained to their petitions (that they'd located with the help of a Strong's Concordance). God answered "Yes" to most of their requests, and when they asked about their prospective mates, He led them to scriptures that taught them what to look for. They also received revelation about asking for things in Jesus' name.

Jesus assured His disciples before He departed that if they asked for anything in His name He would do it. (John 14:14) They knew from John chapter one that Jesus was the Word of God made flesh, so when He encouraged them to ask "in His name," He was simultaneously teaching them that they needed to be "in Him" when they asked to be able to receive; "abiding" in Him, His will, ways and Word.

Asking in His name implied all what they had come to know and understand His name conveyed. Instead of praying that God conform to their wills, they were learning that by conforming to His, He had every intention of prospering and blessing them abundantly.

> *"If you abide in Me, and My words abide in you, you will ask what you desire, and it shall be done for you." (John 15:7)*

CHAPTER 20

"BREAKING BREAD"

Then Jesus lifted up His eyes, and seeing a great multitude coming toward Him, He said to Philip, "Where shall we buy bread, that these may eat?" But this He said to test him, for He Himself knew what He would do. Philip answered Him, "Two hundred denary worth of bread is not sufficient for them, that every one of them may have a little." One of His disciples, Andrew, Simon Peter's brother, said to Him, "There is a lad here who has five barley loaves and two small fish, but what are they among so many?" Then Jesus said, "Make the people sit down." Now there was much grass in the place. So the men sat down, in number about five thousand. And Jesus took the loaves, and when He had given thanks He distributed them to the disciples, and the disciples to those sitting down; and likewise of the fish, as much as they wanted. (John 6:5-11)

Jesus knew what He would do when confronted with the multitudes of hungry men, women, and children, but He wanted to gauge His disciple's growth and challenge their faith and spiritual perceptions. So, He tested them. When Jesus fed the thousands it proved to be a miracle, sign and valuable teaching. The miracle was that He fed thousands with only five loaves of bread and two fish. And He did it twice! (Matthew 15:32-38) Jesus blessed, broke, and then supernaturally multiplied that small amount of food into enough portions to fill thousands of hungry bellies. This had never been done or even heard of before! Miracles had been done in Israel before, but none of this magnitude. Yet, this was only the surface of His divine purpose. Behind the miracle was a sign.

> *And when they found Him on the other side of the sea, they said to Him, "Rabbi, when did you come here?" Jesus answered them and said, " Most assuredly, I say to you, you seek me, not because you saw the signs, but because you ate of the loaves and were filled." (John 6:25, 26)*

So, then, what was the sign of the miracle? It was that through Jesus all provisions could be met. That through Him no man, woman, or child had to go hungry. That by trusting Him, any and all needs could be met. Jesus was disappointed with people, though, because they only sought Him for their immediate, surface (physical) needs. He desired to give them more.

> *"Do not labor for the food which perishes, but for the food which endures to everlasting life, which the Son of Man will give you, because God the Father has set His seal on Him." (John 6:27)*

Jesus was teaching His disciples that He could provide them with a greater and more powerful form of food- spiritual sustenance. He was also teaching them that all provision was attainable through Him, even if it appeared they had insufficient means. That through Him they were fully equipped to meet every need and they were never to send a person in need away. He was showing them that whatever God gave them would always be enough to meet the need and some- even if God had to supernaturally multiply it to make it so. They just had to have faith and trust in Him completely- regardless of what it looked like.

> *But Jesus looked at them and said to them, "With men this is impossible, but with God all things are possible." (Matthew 19:26)*

Living Bread

Now that we have dealt with this miracle and sign in the natural, let us move on to a deeper understanding of this "bread." First, we must establish that physical bread is a mandatory provision of the Father to all whom seek His kingdom first.

> *"Therefore I say to you, do not worry about your life, what you will eat or what you will drink; or about your body, what you will put on. Is not life more than food and the body more than clothing? Therefore do not worry, saying, 'What shall we eat?' or 'What shall we drink?' or 'What shall we wear?' But first seek the kingdom of God and His righteousness, and all these things will be added to you." (Matthew 6:25, 31, and 33)*

Even though most of us are familiar with this passage of Scripture, we find ourselves ignoring (for the most part), or struggling to obey, these instructions (i.e. teachings). Most of us do the opposite and worry, stress over, and pray daily and nightly for both food and clothing (jobs, raises, new school clothes for the kids, rent money, etc.). It seems "right" and "realistic" to us to ask our heavenly Father for our daily/carnal needs (in essence-"worrying" Him about them!).

We may justify our carnal requests with a line out of the prayer that Jesus taught His disciples to pray (what we've coined as 'The Lord's Prayer'). In it, Jesus told them to pray, "Give us this day our daily bread."(Matthew 6:11) So, why would He teach them to pray for their "daily bread," then turn around and tell them not to worry about food at all in the same chapter?! No answer could be clearer than the one He provides in the sixth chapter of John.

> *"I am the bread of life. Your fathers ate the manna in the wilderness, and are dead. This is the bread which comes down from heaven, that one may eat of it and not die. I am the living bread which came down from heaven. If anyone eats of this bread, he will live forever; and the bread that I shall give is my flesh, which I shall give for the life of the world." (John 6:48-51)*

Some of Jesus' disciples were offended and complained about these comments. Jesus tried to clarify His intent and the proper perspective in the following verse:

> *"It is the Spirit who gives life; the flesh profits nothing. The words that I speak to you are spirit, and they are life." (John 6:63)*

Jesus, as vividly and literally as He could, taught us to consume Him. But, even spiritually, how do we eat Jesus?

> *Then Jesus said to them, "Most assuredly, I say to you, unless you eat the flesh of the Son of Man and drink His blood, you have no life in you. Whoever eats my flesh and drinks my*

blood has eternal life, and I will raise him up at the last day. For My flesh is food indeed, and My blood is drink indeed. He who eats My flesh and drinks My blood abides in Me, and I in him. As the living Father sent Me, and I live because if the Father, so he who feeds on Me will live because of Me. This is the bread which came down from heaven-not as your father ate the manna, and are dead. He who eats this bread will live forever."(John 6:53-58)

We must now remember not only who Jesus is (the Son of God), but what Jesus is (the Word of God). We eat Jesus by consuming the word of God. The word of God is "living bread" – our daily spiritual sustenance. Our spirits are our life force, and they need to be well fed-just like our bodies- to remain and operate at optimal health. The nutritional value of physical bread parallels the spiritual bread of life (i.e. Jesus; God's Word); without it our spirits are destitute, weak and hungry. Our spirits are also "thirsty" without spiritual drink-Jesus' blood. This blood cleanses our spirits and allows us to continue partaking of the bread.

Daily Bread

The Word of God is not only provided to sustain our spiritual health, but to guide our very lives. We were originally designed to be in perfect spiritual union with God. This would have made us naturally inclined to lead our lives based on His instructions (i.e. His word). We were created for our Creator to direct our very steps (Proverbs 16:9). This is what the blood of Christ gives us the opportunity to do by restoring us (our spirits) to a clean and pure state. This allows us to reconnect with our Maker/heavenly Father and have intimate communication (communion) once again. Once restored, our responsibility is to feed and strengthen our spirits with God's word, and then learn how to receive and live daily off of it.

"Give us this day our daily bread" is one thing that Jesus taught His disciples to pray for. The entire prayer (i.e. The Lord's Prayer) was designed to instruct them to ask for the things that would make them like Him (or enable them to exist and move in the capacity that He did). Jesus' daily consumption of spiritual bread (God's Word) was mandatory. God's Word dictated everything that He said and did. He did not speak or move without His heavenly instructions.

> *In the meantime His disciples urged Him, saying, "Rabbi, eat." But He said to them, "I have food to eat of which you do not know." Therefore the disciples said to one another, "Has anyone brought Him anything to eat?" Jesus said to them, "My food is to do the will of Him who sent me and to finish His work."(John 4:31-34)*

> *"For I have not spoken on my own authority; but the Father who sent me gave me a command, what I should say and what I should speak. And I know that His command is everlasting life. Therefore, whatever I speak, just as the Father has told me, so I speak." (John 12:49&50)*

> *"Do you not believe that I am in the Father, and the Father in Me? The words that I speak to you I do not speak on my own authority; but the Father who dwells in me does the works." (John 14:10)*

Likewise, we must be able to receive and consume our daily bread (or hear and obey God's word) to be able to accomplish God's will.

You may be thinking that you need to read your Bible more, but receiving your daily bread entails more than that. In all actuality, the Bible is God's word of old; it contains the word that He gave to His people in the past. Coining the Bible as "God's Word" gives the implication that God's Word is finished or completed, though. But that would mean that God has nothing else to say. That 2,000 years ago He wrapped up His entire dialogue with man and just stopped talking. It would make absolutely no sense that the God of the whole universe summed up His entire message to His most prized creation in sixty-six fairly small books. If this were so, why would Jesus instruct His disciples to request their daily bread from the Father? He would have simply instructed them to read the Scriptures.

The Bible (i.e. God's word of old) can definitely aid you in obtaining your daily bread, though. This is how: when you read the Bible, never read with the amount of content in mind. An abundance of words read is irrelevant. The Bible is a spiritual book, and the message God wants to convey to you (the bread that He desires to feed you with) is not relative to the amount of words that you read. You must study with the intent of receiving a personal word from God. To do so, replace any character in any story with yourself, and parallel the circumstances of the passage with your personal situation. Through this, God will allow you to perceive a truth or receive a directive today through what was administered to one of His men or women in times past. For example:

> *Now it happened, on a certain day that He got into a boat with His disciples. And He said to them, "Let us cross over to the other side of the lake." And they launched out. But as they sailed He fell asleep. And a windstorm came down on the lake, and they were filling with water, and were in jeopardy. And they came to Him and awoke Him, saying, "Master, Master,*

> *we are perishing!" Then He arose and rebuked the wind and the raging of the water. And they ceased and there was calm. But He said to them, "Where is your faith?" (Luke 8:22-25)*

First, replace any of the disciples with yourself. The boat in the story can represent being in close proximity, or intimacy, with Jesus. Jesus said, "Let us cross over to the other side of the lake." This can represent a special period or phase during your journey with Jesus, and also His will for you to cross over- or make it through whatever lies before you. Jesus, then, fell asleep, indicating a time period of inaction and non-communication. Then, the storm comes. Replace this literal storm with any type of intense physical or emotional trial or turmoil (infidelity, betrayal, divorce, job loss, poverty, death of a loved one, strife/confrontation, etc.). You turn to your "sleeping" Jesus like the disciples did, in panic to awaken Him; or plead in prayer to God to move on your behalf. Jesus arose, rebuked the storm, and restored the calm-then turned and questioned their faith. How can you apply this? There are countless lessons to glean; countless "words" to receive from on high.

This method of extracting your daily bread from the Bible is an important key. It will train you to be able to receive your daily bread directly from the heavenly bakery. It will train you to hear God's voice. For your daily bread is God's word for you today. Yes-He has a word just for you, just for today. God can speak to you through the Bible, through your experiences, through signs, and people, but His ultimate goal is to speak directly to you through your spirit into your mind. Actually, He has spoken to you directly already, but you probably did not know His voice. This is why you must be trained (or discipled). So you can know His distinct voice. Once you begin to recognize His voice, the Bible will aid you in verifying its authenticity. You do not have to seek confirmation. God will always confirm His word.

While His word for you today may be worded differently, it will never contrast or contradict God's word of old. This is how you know that God is the baker of the new (daily) bread, or how you confirm that He is the source of the "spoken" word (rhema) you have received. If the word aligns with the Scriptures it is of God, but if does not then it is not of God (and it's either from your own mind or from an unclean spirit trying to deceive you). There will come a point when you will no longer need confirmation because you will know His voice, but He will still provide it. But once you know His voice- you know it.

> *"...and the sheep follow him, for they know his voice." (John 10:4)*

> *"My sheep hear My voice, and I know them, and they follow Me." (John 10:27)*

Blessing and Breaking According to the Multitude and Mission

When Jesus blessed and broke the bread to feed the multitudes, He did not attempt to feed them Himself. In Mark 6:39, 40, He commands His disciples to make the people sit down in groups of hundreds and fifties. In the next verse, He blesses and breaks the bread and fish, then gives the food to the disciples to feed the people with. He was training His disciples to administer provision to the people; because fully equipped, completed men of God should be able to bless and break whatever bread (provision) is available to supply the need at hand.

First, the need must be distinguished. Since we know that a man of God's ability to provide physical provision is only a reflection of his spiritual power and authority, let us move onto the more significant bread that he must know how to break; spiritual bread, or the living Word of God. This bread is superior because if it is received and applied, the person's spirit will be impacted, and their external circumstances will change as a result- and to the degree- of their spiritual transformation. His spirit is the source of his positive or negative condition, and to only minister to people's immediate external needs is to minister in part. A man of God will not neglect the greater need.

Jesus ministered to the multitude's spiritual needs before He fed them physically. Through the different accounts in the Gospels, we observe Jesus ministering to different spiritual needs based on the multitude He encountered. Technically, Jesus fed two sets of "multitudes," but the different writers of the Gospels identified four spiritual states Jesus addressed. It's doubtful the writers knew all what the Holy Spirit was pointing out through them, but the different states revealed are noteworthy.

Matthew 14:14 simply says He "healed their sick" before He fed them. Since this passage does not elaborate on their condition beyond them being sick, we perceive that they were completely ignorant as to the cause of their afflictions and, therefore, were simply "sinners," or people who didn't know God and were trapped in their broken and sick states. They did have enough faith to be healed, though, and this group (i.e. sinners) obviously needs Jesus more than ever today.

Mark 6:34 describes the multitude as "sheep not having a shepherd." This depicts a state of being God conscious and willing to serve Him, but unclear as to whom God really is or what kind of service He desires and requires. This class exists today as well, both in and outside of the body of Christ. They need a seasoned man of God in Christ to follow; to direct them to God.

John 6:1-14 highlights a group of "misguided believers." These knew exactly who Jesus was, but they followed Him for what He could do for them vs. what He could do inside of them. They were more concerned with the trinkets in His hand then with who He was. This class is extremely prevalent among believers today. They ask so much from God, but are willing to sacrifice little in return. They would rather act like they don't hear His voice in their hearts, like He requires nothing substantial from them, and like the blood of Christ absolves them from all accountability. These need a man of God to clarify God's word, purpose and focus in their lives.

Lastly, Luke 9:11 depicts Jesus speaking to the people about "the kingdom of God." For Him to break this caliber of spiritual bread with them meant that they were ready to go to the next level. They were "fertile ground," or believers prepared and fully capable of producing fruit at the highest levels. They just needed a sewer and vessel equipped to break the bread of the word and implant it in their hearts and lives.

The Leftover Fragments

> *"So they all ate and were filled, and they took up twelve baskets full of the fragments that remained." (Matthew 14:20)*

In each of the passages where Jesus feeds the multitudes, the disciples picked up baskets full of leftover fragments. This is extremely important with both natural and spiritual bread. Once entrusted with these supernatural keys, God has made a habit of multiplying the provision beyond the need. In the physical this translates into abundance of resource; in the spiritual wisdom and power beyond measure. So, what is the purpose of this excess; these leftover fragments? David proclaimed, "My cup runs over." (Psalms 23:5) The Lord gave Job twice as much as he had before. (Job 42:10)

> *"And I will make your seed as the dust of the earth; so that if a man could number the dust of the earth, then your descendants also could be numbered." (Genesis 13:16)*

> *Now to Him who is able to do exceedingly abundantly above all that we ask or think…. (Ephesians 3:20)*

The disciple of Christ must learn to distribute God's provision according to the need at hand. To feed somebody (physically or spiritually) beyond what they can stomach becomes counter-productive. Once a person is filled, more food loses both its appeal and nutritional (purposeful) value. It is wasteful and unwise to continue to feed physical or spiritual food to a person beyond their capacity.

If this is done with physical provision you risk promoting greed, selfish ambition and misguided motives. The man of God and the children of God must be trained with little before God can trust them with His abundance. This is why Jesus instructed His disciples to sit the multitudes down in fifties and hundreds before He trained them on how to distribute the bread. He had to instruct and entrust His disciples with smaller quantities of bread and people before He sent them to the world.

> *"His lord said to him, 'Well done, good and faithful servant; you were faithful over a few things, I will make you ruler over many things. Enter into the joy of your lord.'"(Matthew 25:21)*

Spiritually, to continue to teach beyond what a student can handle is both a waste of words and (even worse) can confuse the pupil with too much knowledge. We use this principle instituted in almost any academic grade system. We begin educating children with fundamentals, then gradually- as they excel and graduate grades- build upon these fundamentals with more complex teachings and philosophies. Even more so we need to apply this principle to heavenly, eternal truths, and administer (teach) them gradually and wisely. In doing so, the man of God will also have the opportunity to observe and discern the spirit of the hearer; whether genuine or insincere. If the man of God senses ulterior motives he should discontinue his teachings.

> *"Do not give what is holy to the dogs; nor cast your pearls before swine, lest they trample them under their feet, and turn and tear you in pieces." (Matthew 7:6)*

God not only entrusts His chosen vessels to distribute His abundant provision to the needy, but to gather the excess so that nothing is wasted. In the natural, He is entrusting you- not to hoard- but to responsibly oversee and administer this overflow to future needs you may encounter. In the spiritual, He likewise expects you to catalog any overflow of wisdom and insight, then use it to teach and guide His people as future needs present themselves. As stewards of God's kingdom, how we handle the abundance of God's multiplied provision (in both realms) is important.

Do You Get It?

> *Now when His disciples had come to the other side, they had forgotten to take bread. Then Jesus said to them, "Take heed and beware of the leaven of the Pharisees and the Sadducees." And they reasoned among themselves, saying, "It is because we have taken no bread." But Jesus, being aware of it*

said to them, "O you of little faith, why do you reason among yourselves because you have not brought bread? Do you not yet understand, or remember the five loaves of the five thousand and how many baskets you took up? Nor the seven loaves of the four thousand and how many large baskets you took up? How is it you do not understand that I did not speak to you concerning bread?-but to beware of the leaven of the Pharisees and Sadducees." Then they understood that He did not tell them to beware of the leaven of bread, but of the doctrine of the Pharisees and Sadducees. (Matthew 16: 5-12)

The disciples were worried that Jesus was upset because they had forgotten to bring bread with them. This understandably astounded (and probably irritated) Him- they didn't seem to get it! He had fed thousands on two occasions by supernaturally multiplying bread and fish. Why would He care that they failed to bring some bread? His concern was for their spirits and souls- that they could be defiled by the doctrines of men and be rendered ineffective and powerless.

I hope you get it! If you feed your spirit with the true living bread (John 6:48) you will never have to worry about physical sustenance again! God will not only provide for your needs, but provide for all the needs of those who come to you. Others will seek Him through you, and you will be able to produce and provide just like the Master. To do as He did is the hope of your calling.

CHAPTER 21

"You know what?" Rob asked Baron one evening in the recreation building. "I didn't even know what love was!" "Who you telling? Me neither!" Baron shot back.

They had gotten together to study the word, but ended up talking about females and some of their past relationships. In retrospect, they both realized that they had done poorly in that department, and were responsible for causing much pain and heartache. Now in Christ, they shook their heads in shame at their former ways.

"Man, I loved Jessica, but I really carried her through there. I really broke her heart," Rob continued.

"I mean, we could feel the emotion of love, because I know I've been in love before. I just believe that we were incapable of showing it. We knew what it felt like, but we didn't know what it truly was. Or what it demanded of us," Baron added.

They were now in the Spirit; where they needed to be for the Holy Spirit to reveal truth. In their carnal exchanges they saw the things of God as a dull picture; in the Spirit they were in high definition.

"You're right about that. I didn't have a clue," Rob agreed.

"When I think back, even when I looked out for females it was still all about me. My benefit; my pleasure. I knew that whatever I did would pay off at the end of the night, you know? Or at the end of the week, or month- eventually it would pay off."

"I know me- I wasn't trying to take any losses. To put out and get nothing in return? Oh, no! I always calculated what was in it for me."

"It's just. . .I mean- Jesus is the only reason we understand what love is about now. Matter fact, you can't know what love truly means or is apart from Jesus. What He did when He gave His life- that's our paradigm example; the ultimate definition. Without Him you cannot understand that love is about what you can give, not what you can get," Baron expounded.

"Sacrifice! That's the evidence of your love- your sacrifice. What you'll give up."

"Exactly! That's the proof. And not for what you can get in return. The intent must be solely for the person you love. To give them love. To bring them joy. Just for them! That's what Jesus did- He served and gave; gave His life for the world! For God so loved the world. . ."

"That He gave His only begotten Son," Rob interjected. "Gave! Love must give. It cannot be selfish. It must be selfless. Love is not about self. It has nothing to do with you. True love is all about whom you love, and how you can prove it to them."

"I'm sure we're all capable of showing love to some degree, but just not fully without Christ. That's impossible, because He's the model," Baron commented, shaking his head at the implications- that without Christ, man was actually incapable of expressing true, pure love. Rob was stuck in a semi-daze himself as the Holy

Spirit ministered to him. His eyes lit up as more revelation hit him, and he looked over at Baron.

"You know what? Oh. . .wow! Jesus WAS the Father's love!" he exclaimed.

"Yeah. . ." Baron agreed and nodded, not catching the fullness of Rob's revelation.

"No," Rob said with a smirk, shaking his head, "listen- Jesus WAS the Father's love. Not an expression of it. He was literally- the Father's love in the flesh, walking the earth!"

"Yeah," Baron said, jabbing his finger as the puzzle piece fell in place."The Father sent His love, His only begotten Son, into the world. That whomever would believe in His Son- His love- would be saved. To all who would receive His love. Son- love, you can basically use them interchangeably."

"When we receive Jesus, we received the Father's love! That's what saved us, redeemed us, and brought us back from the dead!" Rob exclaimed, and then jumped from his seat. "Oh, my God! The love of God! The love of the Father- that's what defeated the devil's works! That's what overcame death! That's what literally raised Jesus from the dead!"

"And that's what raises us from our dead states. Jesus, the love of God- flowing through our hearts," Baron said, then stood himself and shook his head in astonishment as the Holy Spirit unveiled new truth. "You've got to be kidding me! Hold up- everything Jesus did. . .was love. That's what motivated Him; moved Him; empowered Him! The teachings, the feedings, the healing. . . it was all love!"

"He even gave His own life. The ultimate show of love is self-sacrifice."

"Rob- do you understand how big this is?"

"Do I?! This is the biggest revelation that we've received period!"

Baron shook his head, gazed off and said, "Look, um. . . .This changes everything."

"Listen- everybody knows that Christians are supposed to be about love, but I- personally- don't hear love spoken about that often. I don't hear it preached about like that."

"Man, we've been missing the main thing. That's the single most important piece. The chief cornerstone," Baron said, still shaking his head in a daze. "That's why we have no... power."

"Because we have no love."

They retook their seats and sat in silence for a moment. They both dwelled on the full impact and ramifications of the love revelation. "Love was Jesus' power- how He was able to do the things He did. Love is the most powerful thing- period. Love is God's power in motion. God's power activated. Love is the power source of the kingdom of God," Rob expounded.

"I'm thinking about how powerful even a shadow of love is. Look at gangs. An O.G. can show a shadow of love- smoke some weed with his soldiers and give them some drugs to sell so they can make a few dollars- and they'll kill and put their lives on the line for him. Look how we dealt with females. We just gave them a small piece of love. A tiny slice! Just a glimpse. Bought them a few drinks, a few dates, a few meals, told them some sweet things about how special and beautiful they were, and they gave us everything they held dear in return. Their bodies- everything!"

"That's because we were created in God's image, in His love. We were created to love and be loved, so that's why we can be so easily deceived by anything that even appears to be love. We need love- desperately- and there's so little of it. Look at a child- love is all they need and they can grow up into the greatest human beings."

"And just look at the power only a tiny portion of what looked like love brought us. And that wasn't even real love. Imagine walking in the full power of the love of God!"

"Imagine what we could do. . ." Rob said with a new fire lit in his eyes.

CHAPTER 22

LOVE

"Though I speak with the tongues of men and of angels, but have not love, I have become sounding brass or a clanging cymbal. And though I have the gift of prophecy, and understand all mysteries and all knowledge, and though I have all faith, so that I could remove mountains, but have not love, I am nothing. And though I bestow all my goods to feed the poor, and though I give my body to be burned, but have not love, it profits me nothing." (Corinthians 13:1-3)

The body of Christ has spent an enormous amount of time on everything but love. Who's right and who's wrong, what's "Biblical" and what isn't, who is of God and who is not, can all be determined by the abundance, or lack of, this one word love. The Apostle Paul makes it clear in the verses above that anything we "as Christians" accomplish apart from love is in vain. Everything that the church has written, discovered, built and done has been in vain- in the sight of God- without this single component. One hundred libraries full of philosophies, theologies, commentaries and religious doctrines cannot amount to the power contained in one passage of pure love. The Bible is, indeed, one big love story; a compilation of books chronicling God's love affair with mankind.

God's love is His deepest and richest attribute. Without it He would have been content being alone, but love motivated Him to want to share life with others. Creation itself is the most obvious expression of God's love, because it shows His desire to live in relationship with other things and beings. A loveless God would have been content in His self-existent solitude. Also, to create involves action, and genuine love always motivates and inspires the lover to manifest their love in some form of expression. True love produces.

It has proof. If your love has no evidence it is not true, because it only exists as a feeling- it is in part. Without it being completed through a substantive work, it is not yet love: but rather a sense or feeling of love. Full, whole, actual love must bear fruit of its authenticity. God's own love was made manifest (proven) through the creation of the universe, through mankind, through the earth (created for mankind's habitation and enjoyment), but ultimately through the sacrifice of His Son for the world. Almighty God Himself set love's paradigm standard: love cannot be simply felt and spoken- it must be shown and proven.

Jesus' Love Proven

Jesus was love personified. His ministry was an embodiment of that love; a powerful outward display of who He was internally. As we have established in previous chapters, Jesus' ministry was dual. It consisted of words and works. We will now consider how His works were empowered by love.

When Jesus went out He saw a great multitude; and He was moved with compassion for them, and healed their sick. (Matthew 14:14)

Now Jesus called His disciples to Himself and said, "I have compassion on the multitude, because they have now continued with Me three days and have nothing to eat. I do not want to send them away hungry, lest they faint on the way." (Matthew 15:32)

So Jesus had compassion and touched their eyes. And immediately their eyes received sight, and they followed Him. (Matthew 20:34)

Then Jesus, moved with compassion, stretched out His hand and touched him, and said to him, "I am willing; be cleansed." As soon as He had spoken, immediately the leprosy left him, and he was cleansed. (Mark l: 41, 42)

When the Lord saw her, He had compassion on her and said to her, "Do not weep." Then He came and touched the open coffin, and those who carried him stood still. And he said, "Young man, I say to you, arise." So he who was dead at up and began to speak. And He presented him to his mother. (Luke 7:13-15)

This word "compassion" is translated from a Greek word connoting deep inward pity, sympathy, mercy and affection. It was this compassion- this deeply cultivated, intrinsic love- that enabled Jesus to meet their needs. It's not only that He felt it, but that He felt it strongly enough to inspire Him to act. No healing- no deliverance- no restoration could have taken place without the Messiah's love.

Every single recorded thing Jesus did was motivated by love. Every miracle: multiplying fish and bread to feed the multitudes, all of the healing, calming storms and walking on the sea, raising the dead and restoring the soldier's ear that Peter out off- all of it was one big show of love.

Nobody necessarily deserved it. Most didn't understand it, and those in power hated him for it. He was killed for it. Or, more accurately, He laid down His life for it, for love. Love is the master key! The master key to the kingdom of God. Only with this key can a man unlock the power of God. And only when a man's love is perfected in Christ can he be entrusted with God's power (or be used by God to distribute His power.)

Only with vessels consumed by God's love can God's power be channeled through to the multitudes of people who desperately need it. Jesus knew this, taught it to the disciples, and then commanded them to make more disciples. (Matthew 28:19) They were disciples of love.

> *"A new commandment I give to you, that you love one another; as I have loved you, that you also love one another. By this all will know that you are my disciples, if you have love for one another." (John 13:34, 35)*

Jesus' Love Taught

> *"You have heard that it was said, 'An eye for an eye and a tooth for a tooth.' But I tell you not to resist an evil person. But whoever slaps you on the right cheek, turn the other to him also.*

If anyone wants to sue you and take away your tunic, let him have your cloak also. Whoever compels you to go one mile, go with him two. Give to him who asks you, and from him who wants to borrow from you do not turn away. You have heard that it was said, 'You shall love your neighbor and hate your enemy.' But I say to you, love your enemies, bless those who curse you, do good to those who hate you, and pray for those who spitefully use you and persecute you, that you may be sons of your Father in heaven; for He makes His sun rise on the evil and on the good, and sends rain on the just and on the unjust. For if you love those who love you, what rewards have you? Do not even the tax collectors do the same? If you greet your brethren only, what do you do more than others? Do not even the tax collectors do so? Therefore you shall be perfect, just as your Father in heaven is perfect."(Matthew 5:38-48)

There has been a lot of confusion and debate amongst Christians over Jesus' famous "turn the other cheek" philosophy/teaching. Was He teaching us to literally love our enemies? To literally pray for those who spitefully use us? Literally turn the other cheek if slapped? The answer to all of these questions is a definitive yes. He taught us how to overcome our flesh for ourselves and others by elevating our carnal precepts to Godly standards in the Spirit. He was teaching us how to become "sons of God."(Matthew 5:45)

Instead of engaging this debate, though, let us focus on the Master's intent, which was to establish His disciples in a perfect state of love. We all love those who love us, but union with God (i.e. perfection) demands more. It requires supernatural love; the love of God. This caliber of love extends beyond our carnal ability or sense of reasoning. In other words, it contradicts what we've been taught is "right." This degree of love is based on a higher calling; a bigger purpose wherein our spirits fuse with the Most High's and His love is projected through us.

We are commanded to love our enemies because the wisdom of God shows us that "they know not what they do." (Luke 23:24) In other words, they do not know any better. They have no clue that when they attack and oppose us, they're really attacking and opposing God. But God, in His abundant long suffering and mercy, continues to let the sun rise on them, hoping to disarm and win over even the most evil and hard of heart through the power of His love.

Jesus taught us how to be vessels for God's love to flow through to all (even to the most unrighteous and hateful people of this world). You can be used in this capacity- despite the pain, ridicule, and shame you will undoubtedly experience-once you have risen above yourself and truly answer the highest calling in Christ.

Jesus' emphasis on maintaining this state of love, despite whatever evil or opposition you encounter, was based on His knowledge of God's kingdom. Jesus knew that the power source of God's kingdom was/is love. To operate in the power and authority of this kingdom demanded that He and His disciples be established in love at all times. It is imperative that we remain firmly rooted in love. It must be our encompassing attribute, highest priority and primary motive. It must be our foundation, and this foundation must be maintained at all costs for our heavenly Father's "kingdom to come" and for His "will to be done on earth, as it is in heaven"- through us His sons.

We must be disciplined enough to depend on it, and draw from it, and use it in all circumstances (or people) we may face. The moment we step out of love, we step out of God- out of His spiritual kingdom- and we cut ourselves off from His power. Outside of love, the pure power of God cannot function in and/or through us. Jesus' command to remain in love is for God's love to be able to flow to you (for you) and through you to all who may need it. You are powerless without it. It is essential.

God's power is love. God's love is His power. In the Spirit, the words "love" and "power" are interchangeable. Likewise, our love is our power; our power is our love. Jesus was God's love wrapped in flesh. When we received Him into our hearts we received the Father's love. This was/is the master key to the kingdom- His Son, His love. It's only through Jesus (God's love) that we have access to Him. When we forget about our command and obligation to love, we forget about Jesus- the Author, Finisher and Foundation of our faith. We must not allow our fascination with the manifold jewels in God's kingdom to distract and disconnect us from love. It must be our sustained focal point; His love, our love, love.

"Teacher, which is the great commandment in the law?" Jesus said to him, "You shall love the LORD your God with all your heart, with all your soul, and with your entire mind.' This is the first and great commandment. And the second is like it: 'You shall love your neighbor as yourself.' On these two commandments hang all the Law and the Prophets." (Matthew 22:36-40)

Owe no one anything except to love one another, for he who loves another has fulfilled the law. (Romans 13:8)

And above all things have fervent love for one another, for "Love will cover a multitude of sins."(1 Peter 4:8)

> *But above all things put on love, which is the*
> *bond of perfection. (Colossians 3:14)*

> *Now abide faith, hope, love, these three; but the*
> *greatest of these is love. (1 Corinthians 13: 13)*

Never allow any spiritual experience, insight, or jewel-ANYTHING- to ever eclipse your commitment to, or divert you from, Love. Tap into love and you tap into God. Do not miss the main thing-the whole point! Without love you have nothing in God. Without love your words and works lack God and life. Even if the words are for or about God, he is not in them.

> *"But woe to you Pharisees! For you tithe mint*
> *and rue and all manner of herbs, and pass by*
> *justice and the love of God. These you ought to*
> *have done without leaving the others undone."*
> *(Luke 11:42)*

Without love we cannot do what God has called us to do; our purposes cannot be fulfilled. Everything you have labored for and learned thus far, in your life and from the pages of this book, has led up to this point- this one revelation. If you have been wondering why the power of God seems to be absent in your life, you have now been given the answer and the access key.

> *Beloved, let us love one another, for love is of*
> *God; and everyone who loves is born of God and*
> *knows God. He who does not love does not know*
> *God, for God is love. (1 John 4: 7, 8)*

No Longer In Part

First Corinthians chapter thirteen has been coined "the love chapter." In it are thirteen verses wherein Paul expounds on love.

The first three verses teach that spiritual gifts profit nothing if love is absent. The next four verses give a detailed description of love's attributes; a specific definition of what pure, undefiled love looks like in its perfected form. The next five verses often get taken out of context because they don't seem to directly relate, but this is an error. 1 Corinthians 13 is indeed the love chapter, and what the Holy Spirit conveys about love in these verses is profound. Let's start with the first three (of the last six verses).

> *Love never fails. But whether there are prophecies, they will fail; whether there are tongues, they will cease; whether there is knowledge, it will vanish away. For we know in part and we prophesy in part. But when that which is perfect has come, then that which is in part will be done away. (1 Corinthians 13:8-10)*

Wow: love never fails! This is pure, genuine love's record: undefeated. This is also an indictment of every church minister. Paul's apostolic anointing was full and complete. He fed the sheep God gave him, proclaimed the gospel in boldness, and opposed Satan's kingdom by displaying God's in power and authority. But he also witnessed a clear lack of power and authority within the lives and ministries of other believers. Prophecies, tongues, and knowledge all "in part." And the Holy Spirit revealed exactly why their fruit was partial.

Their fruit was partial and incomplete because it was not fully matured. Their gifts were of God but not in full. They were undependable and inconsistent. The same is evident in today's church. Most know somebody that knows of somebody who was "supposedly" healed. Glimpses of kingdom power can be seen during certain Spirit-filled revivals or worship services. All-in-all, though, what we behold is definitely in part.

But they, and we, were assured in Verse 10 that "when that which is perfect has come, then that which is in part will be done away with." We have already established in the twelfth chapter that "perfect" in the original Greek means complete, of full age or fully matured. So, then, what is Paul referring to when he writes, "when that which is perfect has come"? The Holy Spirit was conveying that a lack of genuine, pure love was the source of their inconsistencies and failures.

Let us be clear- God can obviously use anybody (man, woman or child) at any time to accomplish His purposes. He is God Almighty and can do as He pleases. However, we are focusing on our responsibility because it has been God's custom to make His power manifest and available to His people through His people.

As we grow in Christ, we yearn to be used by our heavenly Father- for His kingdom, for the benefit of others, and for the confirmation of the gospel message we preach. For God to use us in full kingdom power and authority takes maturation, and there is nothing that must be developed more in the servant of God than love. He uses all of His children to a certain extent (in part), but only full grown men and women of God are empowered to walk in complete, unfailing dependability.

Our spiritual maturity is based on the condition of our hearts- namely, in what capacity we love. This applies first to God, then to man who was created in God's image. This is God's gauge of our growth, and should be how we measure each other's as well. How does he or she love and how much? This is how God determines what to feed us, and how much He can advance us. All of the pruning, molding, and refining by fire is for love. It's all about growth.

> *When I was a child, I spoke as a child, I understood as a child, I thought as a child;*

> *but when I became a man, I put away childish*
> *things. (1 Corinthians 13:11)*

The maturation process of love is referred to once again here in this verse. The "child" in this verse represents the children of God who, because of their spiritual youth, do not comprehend the paramount significance of love. Paul admitted here that he himself was once a child in the Spirit, but when he "became a man" he put away "childish things." In essence, the spiritually mature come to understand that nothing is more critical or essential than love. When Paul grew up (spiritually) he reached a point where he understood that love was the ground wire that supplied the power to everything else in his walk with God.

> *For now we see in a mirror, dimly, but then face*
> *to face. Now I know in part, but then I shall know*
> *just as I also am known. (Corinthians 13:12)*

Once love has been perfected in you, your spiritual vision will be enhanced. You will be able to see yourself clearly through the eyes of God, and no longer through your own dim, distorted misperceptions. You will finally be able to see and love yourself as God sees and loves you. This perfected love will also enable you to do the same with others- see and love them as God does. You will finally be able to fully embrace and love and be confident in yourself, and help others to do the same. For the second greatest commandment is to "love thy neighbor as thyself," but how can you love your neighbor if you've never grown to love yourself?

Blood Clots

> *"I do not pray for these alone, but also for those*
> *who will believe in Me through their word; that*
> *they all may be one, as You, Father, are in Me,*

and I in You; that they also may be one in Us, that the world may believe that You sent Me."
(John 17:20&21)

Thereisonebodyandone Spirit...(Ephesians4:4)

From whom the whole body, joined and knit together by what every joint supplies, according to the effective working by which every part does its share, causes growth of the body for the edifying of itself in love.(Ephesians 4:16)

The corporate body of believers in Christ is supposed to function as one living organism- one body. The world is supposed to be able to look at the church as a living witness and testimony of Jesus` love and power. The church is supposed to be a magnified, multiplied reflection of Jesus Himself, and the multitudes should be drawn to the mercy, compassion and healing touch of the church, just as they were drawn to His. While millions flock to our churches for guidance and comfort, there is a clear lack of love in the body of Christ in this day and age.

The body has become severely fragmented for a whole host of reasons. Some are understandable, but others are simply not of God. Many Christians come from different social, economic, and cultural backgrounds, and are therefore more comfortable worshipping, studying, and hearing God's word preached and taught in different styles. We use "styles" and not "ways" because our concern should be to serve God in whatever way that He pleases. But if He tells us to worship Him, we presumably reserve the option to do it quietly or loudly, or whichever ministry style the flock at hand is most receptive to.

When it comes to preaching/teaching, some prefer a more theology-based or seminary-structured formal approach, while others a more liberal or spirit-driven, animated, passionate one. These preferences display the wide and diverse spectrum of people within the national, and global, Christian community. These diversities are harmless if our appointed shepherds intentionally encourage and promote unity and love towards each other beyond these superficial boundaries, and make a concerted effort to fellowship and mingle with various congregations within the fold.

This is tough, though, when the main divisive element in the body of Christ today is doctrine. Right or wrong, religious doctrine has been the primary source of division and fragmentation within the body of Christ since the church began. If we, as believers, truly exist as one body, then doctrines are our blood clots. Just as blood must circulate throughout the human body, love must circulate freely within the body of Christ for it to be healthy and effective; to operate at an optimum level. These blood clots have crippled the body of Christ, diminishing its corporate power and stagnating many of its individual members. The body of Christ is a mere shadow of what it will be when united in love.

Correct, Biblical doctrine does have its place, however. The question is what point do we draw the line of separation when it comes to false doctrine? Or, better yet, what constitutes one as "my brother"?

> *By this you know the spirit of God: every spirit that confesses that Jesus Christ has come in the flesh is of God, and every spirit that does not confess that Jesus has come in the flesh is not of God. (John 4:23)*

Most doctrinal differences come from Scriptures that can validly be perceived in different ways. A heavenly word, when sent down to earth, may be interpreted numerous ways; one word from the mouth of God may easily be equivalent to an entire book of earthly words. He is that much higher! This passage is clear, though. First of all, "Christ" is translated "Messiah," so confession that Jesus is the Messiah (i.e. Christ), and that He came in the flesh as a Man is a must. To believe that He was anything less than Christ, or to believe that He came as anything other than "Man," are doctrinal fundamentals that must be agreed upon.

Whoever confesses that Jesus is the Son of God, God abides in him, and he in God. (John 4:15)

That if you confess with your mouth the Lord Jesus and believe in your heart that God has raised Him from the dead, you will be saved. (Romans 10:9)

A confession in Christ should establish one's belief that the Son of God- Jesus- was sent into the world as a Man to save us through His blood sacrifice and give us the words that lead to eternal life. Believing in His resurrection- that He rose on the third day- completes this confession that He "is" Lord. If He never rose, He died and only "was" Lord. Jesus Christ of Nazareth- the Messiah sent from God- must live and reign as Lord and Savior in the heart of the believer.

Scripture demands no other doctrinal fundamentals that we- as disciples of Christ- must agree on. The Father touched our hearts at some point, and allowed us to grasp the reality of Jesus and what was done through Him for us. (Matthew 11:27) If we received this gift through faith, we received spiritual redemption, restoration and the salvation of our souls. We didn't know the intricacies of proper theological Christian doctrine! We simply knew that He, and the stories about Him, were real, and that He was calling for us. Any other Scriptural passages that can feasibly be interpreted in different ways are not valid ground to disassociate, separate, and cause schism in the body of Christ. This separation, promulgated through dogma and religious doctrine and tradition, is not of God.

It breeds contempt and misjudgment, and promotes religious and sectarian superiority. It is of the evil one. It has stopped the love (blood) from flowing freely throughout the body of believers in Christ. When you receive Jesus, you receive the love of God inside of you. When the next man/woman receives Him they receive the same. When you separate from your brother/sister, you separate yourself from the love of God inside of him/her and separate him/her from the love of God inside of you. This separation of love is a separation of power. This brings to mind the famous military strategy- "divide and conquer." This division makes us weak. Jesus foreknew how important it would be for us to be bonded in love, so before He departed He demanded it.

> *"A new commandment I give to you, that you love one another; as I have loved you, that you also love one another." (John 13:34)*

> *"This is my commandment, that you love one another as I have loved you." (John 15:12)*

> *"These things I command you, that you love one another." (John 15:17)*

This new commandment to love your brother is actually the fulfillment of an old one. The Leviticus law states that, "You shall not hate your brother in your heart."(Leviticus 19:17) This was before Jesus made a way for the Holy Spirit to indwell man, though. Through Christ, God Himself actually lives inside of your brother, so the commandment to love your brother is now a fulfillment of the first and greatest commandment- to love God!

If someone says, "I love God," and hates his brother, he is a liar; for he who does not love his brother whom he has seen, how can he love God whom he has not seen? And this commandment we have from Him: that he who loves God must love his brother also. (1 John 4:20, 21)

CHAPTER 23

Baron and Rob knew what they had to do. It was clear as day. God was calling His body to love. The spiritual state that they were operating in was insufficient. The Spirit of God was there, but the love was not circulating in the body. There were too many blood clots. The body was in need of healing. It was ineffective in its current state. It lacked authority, and it lacked power. It was dysfunctional; sick; impaired. It was in a "dead" state. But if the love of the Father raised Jesus from the grave, it could certainly raise the body of Christ at Butner.

There were numerous brothers who held different Bible studies but didn't attend the main church services on Sundays. There were Jehovah's Witnesses, Catholics, and Messianics all on the compound. Baron and Rob didn't have a detailed plan, but they felt it would be wise and orderly to spread God's love message to the ministers first, then work their way around to the rest of the members of the church.

Baron wasted no time inviting a group of the more visible, outspoken brothers to meet with them after dinner the following evening. They met around a table on the yard. Not counting Baron, there were eight others present. Baron kept looking for Rob, but he was nowhere to be found. Time was ticking, and he decided to get started. He asked one of the older brothers to open up with a word of prayer, and then he began.

"God has sent me with a message, and that's why I called this meeting. I thank you brothers for making time for this with such short notice. I would like to start off with a couple of apologies.

"Alex, I never really said anything bad about you, but I have listened to and entertained some negative gossip about you, and some of the ways different guys said you've conducted yourself. I hadn't even met you at the time, and I thought this was okay because they were just opinions, but I was wrong. I should have silenced it, or departed from it, as soon as I heard it, because you're my brother in Christ. So- do you forgive me?"

Alex was sitting right next to Baron, and after considering for a brief moment he nodded his approval. "Yeah, I forgive you, little brother."

Baron then turned to another elder brother, one of the lead choir members. "Brother Moreland, I've spoken to you a few times in passing, but you always looked mean and you barely spoke back. Although I kept greeting you, I voiced my disdain towards what I looked at as an attitude from you. I shouldn't have said a word about you to anybody else, because you're my brother. So I apologize to you as well."

"I accept your apology, young brother. Um- just so you know- I've been in a lot of bad situations, so I just try to be careful and cautious in this environment. So many guys in this place have so many things going on, and you never know what you're dealing with when you cross somebody's path. So, I just try to stay in my lane, and try my best to remain humble. I don't mean to come off any certain kind of way, but I guess that's just how I am," Brother Moreland replied.

Almost everybody had brought their Bibles along, and Baron proceeded to lead them to the different Scriptural passages that the Holy Spirit had highlighted to them about love. Everything went fine until he breached the issue of doctrine. When Baron began telling them that the doctrinal separation and the strife and division it caused was not of God, and that all who believed that Jesus was the Son of God sent to die for their sins was their brother, confusion erupted! Rob had been on an unexpected visit, and arrived in the midst of the controversy.

"That Messianic stuff is just not Scriptural! If you are trying to live by the law in anyway then you might as well be a Jew! How can I sit here and call you my brother?! I don't believe in that stuff!" Alex stated adamantly.

Rob closed his eyes and started praying in the Spirit as the debate gained traction. He could sense the enemy's presence, and came against the kingdom of darkness in the spirit realm. Baron continued to try to keep the attitudes and emotions in check, and encouraged everybody to express their viewpoints respectfully because there were members from various denominations present. Irritation and frustration continued to build.

Suddenly, Rob threw his hands up, and said, "Brothers- listen! We are here to establish love. Not to argue and debate about different doctrinal beliefs. It is the main reason the body is separated; the reason the love is not flowing! So, please, let us get back to the point that we're all here for- and that's love!"

The meeting eventually ended on a cordial note, although it had played out far differently than what Rob and Baron had expected. There was no way in a million years they would have imagined a "love message" igniting so much conflict amongst a group of Christians. The push back was significant, and they had never experienced that level of opposition. They realized, then, that the mission was going to be tougher than what they imagined. They continued to call different groups of ministers and leading members together to spread the word that God had sent them with. Most signed on, believed the call to love in a broader and greater capacity was of God, and gave their support. The opposition continued to come from one specific group, though, and they eventually identified them as "the elders"- i.e. the older brothers. Baron and Rob were determined to do God's will, though, and would not be dismayed. Their minds were made up to do what God had sent them to do.

Once they spread this word amongst the leadership, God instructed them to bring it to the whole body, collectively, at one time. They went to God for instructions on how to do this, because the F.B.O.P. did not permit gatherings on the yard beyond a few individuals for fear of riots, gang wars, or rebellious demonstrations. So they wouldn't be able to call the entire body on the yard at any one time. God gave them a word- "Chaplain." So, they went to speak to the chaplain.

Although they were somewhat skeptical and apprehensive, they met with the chaplain one afternoon and expounded on the word God had given them about love in-depth. The chaplain described the message as "the beat of his own heart," and gave them a date to present it before the church. It was two weeks away.

CHAPTER 24

"PERFECTING PHILEO"

Love emanates (or flows out) from one of two sources: the soul or spirit. It is human nature to love from the soul. This love originates in the mind and/or emotions. Any form of soulful love is derived from the Greek word "Phileo," and can be classified under some variation of this root word.

Phileo love is based on affections and/or attractions. It spans from the love of good men, to brotherly love, to the love of money, to love in marriage, to loving God, to the love of a friend, etc.etc. From 'philosophy'(the love of wise things) to 'Philadelphia' (love of the brethren), Phileo is the root word describing any love based on personal attachment, preference, attraction and/or affection towards individuals or objects one is fond of.

Phileo-based love can be superficial (philedonos: lover of pleasure) or extremely deep (phíloteknos: the maternal love of one's children). It can be wonderful and feel great, or it can feel treacherous and turn deadly, because its stability is based on some degree of expectation. The cliché, "There's a thin line between love and hate," is in regard to Phileo-based love. Phileo is the human, lower manifestation and reflection of love.

Agape is the higher, heavenly form of love that is rooted in the Spirit. Only through God can a human love in the capacity of agape. Agape is rooted in an obligation based on a principle. For instance, agape motivated our heavenly Father to send His only begotten Son to die for a distorted, perverted, wayward mankind. God felt obligated to love and provide for a disobedient, contrary creation based on the sole principle that He created us. This love was not based on our performance or His preference.

This is agape. And agape is perfect. Agape is unconditional because it cannot be earned, altered or regulated by its recipient. It exists solely in the heart and spirit of its possessor, and its intent is completely selfless. It can only produce benefit and provision. Agape's primary objective is to fill any need it identifies within the scope of its compassion. To be on the receiving end of agape is to experience pure, untainted, unconditional love.

Agape is love in its highest, perfected form. It is the fully matured, purified love of God. The fully evolved, spiritual pinnacle that only God can transmute and birth in the hearts of men. The Father's main focus is our heart because His power is agape, and only through earthen vessels consumed by agape can His supernatural power be channeled through to this world. A purified heart in man is what the copper is within the electrical wire: the actual conduit for power (God's agape) to travel through.

The writer's of the Gospels repeatedly wrote that Jesus was "moved with compassion" before God's power was made manifest for miraculous healings and provision. Compassion is agape's primary trait, as agape is always seeking to meet a need. Jesus walked in agape continually during His earthly ministry, and it is the Holy Spirit's goal for all of Jesus' disciples to attain this state.

CHAPTER 25

Baron and Rob received a word from on high. It was that they would need more brothers- more power- to establish love in the body during the love service. They didn't know why they weren't enough, but chose not to question God. If He said they needed more for the mission- they needed more.

They composed a makeshift list of all of the brothers who had appeared to be moved by the love message God had sent them with. The list came up to twelve men, most of who ministered to the body at Butner in some form or capacity. One of the twelve, a brother named Anthony, expounded on the spiritual significance of the number twelve: there were twelve sons of Jacob, twelve tribes of Israel, and twelve disciples. Twelve seemed to represent order; a number that God used to establish His structures upon.

After the number was confirmed, they began to approach the different individuals on the list to get more clarity and a firmer affirmation of their stances on the love ministry. Some quickly backed out because they couldn't truly swallow crossing doctrinal barriers. It was obviously easier said than done, and now that they were being asked to be a part of doing it, they could no longer mask their inability to love and accept those outside their denominational parameters as brothers.

Their numbers dropped down to nine, then to eight, then back up to eleven. They were forced to meet and make progress with whomever God gave them. There were certain gifts that Baron and Rob wanted to move in (like healing and seeing God's power made manifest based on the things they had learned), but they received another clear word- "Wait." Rob was then led to look in the book of Acts where he immediately came across Jesus instructing the apostles to wait in chapter one verse four. They did so in the upper room and verse fourteen says that they, "all continued while they waited, with one accord in prayer and supplication."

They recognized the parallel, and believed God was giving them an opportunity to get on one accord with the twelve in preparation for the love service. That's when the elders really started attacking Baron and Rob. A lot of offensive, nasty comments and ridicule made its way back to them, and other attacks were blatant- face to face. Brothers who had initially embraced them in love and fellowship turned completely against them, and accused them of watering down the gospel and spreading false doctrine.

Alex initially got on board with the twelve, but eventually made some contrary remarks that came to the light, and led Baron and Rob to question his intentions. When they confronted him, seeking clarity, he erupted. It turned out that he had never truly overcome his dogmatic perceptions. He went on to call their ministry soft and labeled them novices. Raised a charismatic Pentecostal, he proclaimed that Baron did not have the Spirit because he didn't speak in tongues. Now separated from them, he seemed intent on leading some kind of crusade against them.

Brothers continued to bring more reports of other brothers criticizing and vilifying them. Rob had experienced a form of persecution for righteousness sake in the past when he broke his ties with his former gang for Christ. Baron got his taste from having to swallow his pride on numerous occasions for Christ's name sake, and dealing with the sly comments and backlash that comes with taking the higher road. Still, neither had been previously persecuted solely for speaking God's word and doing His will, and neither had experienced it from within the Christian community. This was their first time being attacked by brothers, but it was through these brothers that they began to understand what they were dealing with.

First of all, the opposition was coming from all brothers who held leadership positions and ministered to the body. They didn't know if that meant anything, but it was actually all of the elders who seemed to be against them. Next, they recognized that the primary source of contention was definitely doctrinal.

Lastly, they encountered the same nasty, arrogant and slanderous reaction from all of their attackers. This led them to one conclusion: they were dealing with some sort of evil spirit (or maybe a group of them on one specific assignment). They sought God for answers.

They began rebuking these unclean spirits in prayer, but could only vaguely identify them based on the traits they'd recognized. It was on Baron's heart to seek a name, and he lay on his bed one restless night asking God to reveal it. He had read somewhere that in ancient days, they believed that you had to have knowledge of a spirit's name to gain control over it. He no longer believed that referencing this spirit's attributes or referring to it in general was sufficient to be able to bind and cast it from their midst. A name coalesced clear as day in his mind's eye: "Molech."

He vaguely remembered seeing the name in the Old Testament somewhere, but he didn't want to get up and search then because it was in the middle of the night and his cell mate was asleep. He made a mental note to write the name down in the morning.

As he got ready for work the following morning he remembered about Molech. He retrieved his concordance, and looked up the name. He didn't have time to look up the definition, so he just wrote down the name and the few scriptures it was located in on a small piece of paper, then left for work. He usually bumped into Rob on his way to work, and that morning was no different. He handed the piece of paper to Rob, and asked him to do some research on it while he was at work.

Molech turned out to be an Old Testament idol that repeatedly made its way into the temple of God (YHWH). It had the face of a calf or ram, and had outstretched arms. The idol was heated with fire from the inside, and the priests encouraged the people to "pass their children through the fire," or sacrifice them to Molech. This meant sitting the babies on the heated, outstretched arms of the idol while other priests beat loudly on drums to drown out the cries of their children being burned to death.

Molech, when translated, literally means "king." With all of this information, they were able to connect the dots and make the parallels. Molech was of course a physical idol, but there were obviously demonic spirits that were operating through the priests (or "kings") to promote this idol to the Israelites. These spirits were crafty and ruthless enough to get God's people to sacrifice their own children to be burned to death!

These same evil spirits were at play in God's modern-day temple- the church- and had infiltrated primarily through the doorway of doctrine. These cunning spirits were now influencing the modern-day priests- pastors, ministers and (yep!) elders- to offer up the "children of God"(the body of believers) on the altar of the idol of religious doctrine. Man's allegiance to their concepts and perceptions of Scripture would now take precedence over the supreme and greatest commandment of God- which was/ is to love. The demons had gotten stealthier and changed the appearance of the idol, but they had still gotten it into the temple, and the effects were still detrimental.

Now that the Holy Spirit had revealed their enemy's identity, they took this knowledge to the twelve. The twelve were instructed to surround the body during the love service for two functions: first to oppose, bind, and cast out all unclean spirits operating according to the order of Molech, and then to loose and empower the congregation to walk freely in the power of love. To accomplish either, each member had to have already been moved by the love of God to tear down their own internal prejudices and walls of separation (mentally and spiritually) that had previously prevented them from loving other believers. This qualified them as willing vessels for this specific commission: infusing the body of Christ at Butner with love (blood).

CHAPTER 26

"DOORWAYS"

> *"When an unclean spirit goes out of a man,*
> *he goes through dry places, seeking rest; and*
> *finding none, he says, 'I will return to my house*
> *from which I came.'" (Luke 11:24)*

> *Jesus answered and said to him, "If anyone*
> *loves me, he will keep my word; and My Father*
> *will love him, and we will come to him and make*
> *our home with him." (John 14:23)*

In both of these passages, Jesus referred to man as a house (home, abode, etc). The first dealt with the indwelling of unclean spirits in man, while the second dealt with the indwelling of Jesus' Spirit and the Father's. If man is a "house," then the exterior of the home would be his physical body; the interior his soul and spirit. And we all know the most normal way to enter a home is through a door.

The doorways to the inner man are the mouth, nose, eyes, ears, and skin. It is through these five entry points that the soul and spirit can be influenced by the outside world. These five senses are how we receive a "sense" of what's going on around us. Man's body literally houses his soul and spirit. Through the body, the soul and the spirit-man can be either corrupted or edified (leading to damnation or glory).

The spirit realm (consisting of God, the devil and their respective kingdoms) are vying for (or warring over) the possession of "houses." More specifically, they're fighting over the spoils within these houses (i.e. the souls and spirits of men). The stage has been set, and both sides have equal opportunity to access and try to win over the hearts of the men. They both enter and display what their kingdoms have to offer through the same doorways. The things of God's kingdom are evident: they are pure, righteous, holy, and full of love, hope and virtue. In contrast, the things of Satan's kingdom are all lustful and passion-fueled, instant and self- gratifying yet fleeting and insatiable; heartless, greedy, and evil.

When anything from either kingdom enters any door, its first stop is man's soul. After he hears, smells, sees, tastes, or feels a thing it then registers in his mind or emotions (or both).It looks to influence and sway him one way or the other. Neither side can directly control man because man has been given free-will. He is constantly faced with a choice to make based on what enters his doors. Man eventually "makes up his mind" based on the condition of his heart. If his heart is for God, his ultimate decision will be godly. This will evidence his allegiance to God's kingdom. Likewise, if his heart has been corrupted by the evil one his decision will reflect that.

> *"A good man out of the good treasure of his heart brings forth good things, and an evil man out of the evil treasure brings forth evil things." (Matthew 12:35)*

> *"You will know them by their fruits. Do men gather grapes from thorn bushes or figs from*

thistles? Even so, every good tree bears good
fruit, but a bad tree bears bad fruit. Every tree
that does not bear good fruit is cut down and
thrown into the fire. Therefore by their fruits
you will know them." (Matthew 7:16-20)

Make no mistake- man's "works" (his choices, decisions, the fruits
he bears) proves whom he serves. It starts with belief, but ends
with action. What you truly believe eventually flows out. Belief
alone is not enough!

"Thus faith by itself, if it does not have works,
is dead" (James 2:17)

"You believe that there is one God. You do well.
Even the demons believe and tremble!' (James
2:19)

Belief begins in the mind, but until it penetrates the heart it
won't be evident in one's actions. You can believe in God, but still
choose to serve the devil. If you are not extremely careful you can
serve the devil without even knowing it.

"You do the deeds of your father." Then they
said to Him, "We were not born of fornication,
we have one Father-God." Jesus said to them,
"If God were your Father, you would love Me, for
I proceeded forth and came from God; nor have
I come of Myself, but He sent me. Why do you
not understand my speech? Because you are
not able to listen to My word. You are of your
father the devil, and the desires of your father
you want to do." (John 8: 41-44)

We see, here, Jesus telling certain Jews that the devil was their father based on their deeds and inability to understand His word. They played the "race card"- claiming that Abraham was their father based on their Jewish heritage. (John 8:34) Jesus came to bring the law and our understandings to spiritual fulfillment. In the Old Testament, God established His covenant with one nation established by race and custom. In the New Testament, God extends this covenant to a nation of believers- called to believe in His Son, and chosen based on their desire to overcome evil with good. (1 Cor. 12:13) There is no free pass into God's kingdom based on bloodline, position, or heritage. Although they claimed that God was their father, Jesus exposed their spiritual allegiance based their words, works, and fruits.

The goal of both spiritual kingdoms is the same- to penetrate to the heart of man. A man's words and works evidence which kingdom he serves, and who has conquered his heart. It's that simple. The ultimate goal, however, is to penetrate men so deeply that they are consumed. The kingdom of God seeks to consume a man with good and vice versa. Only a completely consumed man can be fully used by either kingdom.

Both God and the devil, and their respective kingdoms, are spirit, and it is only when a man's allegiance penetrates past his soul to his spirit-man that he is fully accessible and usable to the spirit realm. Only in this state can supernatural, spiritual power be directly transferred through him to effect people or circumstances in this world. These fully consumed men and women are the fulltime, sold out worshippers of either God or the devil.

As long as a man's heart is split between good and evil, in any degree, he can only be used in part for either kingdom, and he remains vulnerable. He can still be swayed in either direction. When a man is completely consumed, his mind and heart are fixed, and there is no more room for compromise. His master has been chosen.

In conclusion, no responsible person allows any and everybody into their home. In it is most, if not all, of their valuable possessions. They certainly wouldn't allow anybody in whom they knew had ill motives or intent. Well, even more so, your physical body is your most immediate house. Within it are your life's sacred and eternal components- your soul and spirit. Anything that enters the doorway of your body is seeking intimate fellowship with the core of your nature. No matter how trivial or mundane a thing may be, it is worth it to evaluate and monitor anything you entertain or intake. Depending on its source, it could be hugely beneficial or detrimental. You must be watchful and disciplined with what you allow inside of you if you truly value your internal, spiritual well-being.

> *Be sober; be vigilant because your adversary, the devil, walks about like a roaring lion, seeking whom he can devour. (1 Peter 5:8)*
>
> *"The thief does not come except to steal, to kill, and to destroy." (John10:10)*
>
> *Now the serpent was more cunning than any beast of the field which the Lord God had made... (Genesis 3:1)*

CHAPTER 27

Rob and Baron had started attending the Christian Spanish services on Sundays at 1:30 in the afternoon. There were some strong brothers in the Latino community, and their love ministry mandated that they cross all boundaries within the body of Christ. That included the language barrier. With the help of an interpreter, they were received warmly and had chosen to attend their services (which were actually bilingual with the help of a weekly, visiting interpreter from the outside) to support their proclamation of love.

Rob attended one particular Sunday service alone, because Baron happened to be in visitation. They were still facing harsh opposition led by Alex, and a group of their attackers had approached the members of the Spanish congregation in an effort to discredit Baron and Rob. The primary leader/elder of the Spanish congregation- a brother named Danny- opened with prayer then opened his Bible to read some opening scriptures, as was their custom. He went straight to a couple of the main passages Baron and Rob had been using to spread the love message. Alex, suddenly, sprung to his feet enthusiastically!

"See! I told you so! Confirmation, confirmation! "Alex hollered excitedly, and started jabbing his finger at different brothers.

Rob's insides felt like they were being torn apart, and he dropped and shook his head. He wasn't sure what exactly was being conveyed, but Alex had pitted himself against them, so whatever he was claiming was being "confirmed" was surely some attack or accusation against them. What made it really terrible was that he was using the same scriptures God had given them, against them, somehow! It was a classic satanic play- use God's own word, slightly altered, against His purpose. (Genesis 17 and 3:1)

Rob was disgusted. He wanted to leave. He still couldn't believe his own brothers were coming against him, and now they were trying to make some sort of open spectacle of him. What had he done to deserve this? He had only done what God told him to do: which was to enlighten the body with a deeper revelation of, and commitment to, love. How could that be misconstrued? He hadn't tried to exalt himself in any way, and he had no ulterior motives. He had gained nothing from it. He'd simply been obedient.

He'd done it out of his love for God and his brothers. It had all been done in love. "Why are you allowing this to happen? What's going on?" Rob asked God.

"How was My love displayed to the world?" was the question that God answered him with.

Rob pondered the question as the spiritual attack ensued. The answer suddenly came to him. What was the greatest display of God's love to the world? Giving His Son to be crucified. The slander, the accusations, the lies, the mockery, the physical abuse and shame, then ultimately His death- it was all the love of the Father made manifest. It was manifested through pain. In the face of man's worst potential- through the condemnation and murder of an innocent Man.

In the face of the devil's hate, God secured His most significant victory through the devil's ruthless, hate-filled plot. Had Jesus never sacrificed His life, generations of sinners around the globe would had never had the opportunity to be redeemed by His blood, reconnected to the Father, and restored in the power of the Spirit. Rob received the revelation of co-crucifixion.

God was calling for his life. He was calling him to death. Not physically- Jesus had done that already- but a type of death all the same. A death to himself, to his pride, to his identity while saving the world. A death to his personal goals, desires, to his carnality. God wanted to know if He ripped everything away from Rob, would he still be obedient. Would he still serve Him? Even to death?

The concept crushed him. He was already incarcerated. Then even more limited based on his personal self-denial and sacrifice to God. Then always slightly wounded, having to constantly swallow his pride as a "humble disciple"- then this. The reality of all he was going through overwhelmed him. It all really made perfect sense, but it was still extremely hard to justify. That's when he remembered who Jesus suffered at the hands of- His own brethren, the Jews.

Rob felt like he had been put in a position to make a decision right then and there. Would he live or would he die."For whoever desires to save his life will lose it, but whoever loses his life for my sake will save it."(Luke 9:24)

Tears slipped from his eyes. Rob revisited the terrible steps that led to Jesus' crucifixion, and then contemplated his own willingness to be sacrificed for the kingdom of God. Would he sacrifice himself for the Father and for Jesus? Was he really willing to see this thing through to the end or not? He, then, made up his mind. This was what had to be done. For this world to experience the pure and powerful love of the Father, the lives of His sons had to be given. It was the only way.

"I will," Rob said, "I'll do it, Father."

* * *

Baron strutted to the chow-hall feeling great that evening. His visit with Tish that day was wonderful. No arguments or strife. He helped her with some spiritual issues, they prayed together, took some pictures, laughed and shared a whole lot of love. It seemed like they were, once again, on the right track. They were growing very close.

As he neared the front of the line, a female lieutenant informed him that he needed to report to the lieutenant's office after he ate. He knew that it couldn't be for anything good.

"For what?" Baron asked.

She replied. "You caught a disciplinary shot."

"What?! I haven't done anything! What could I possibly have a write-up for?"

"Ms. Brown wrote you up in visitation earlier for touching your female's rear end. She gave you a sex charge." Baron was devastated.

Inmates could only embrace their visitors once when they arrived, and once when they departed. He had been involved with Tish for so long that rubbing her backside briefly as they kissed had become practically a ritual before they parted ways. He never got excessive, but she was his fiancé. Officers had barely commented to him at all about the nature of his embraces over the span of hi years incarcerated.

Although Ms. Brown had been a source of frustration for him with his visits since he'd been at Butner, he couldn't believe she had gone that far. He had never- ever- heard of one case of an inmate losing something as precious as his visits over such a minor offense. The most that visitation officers would do normally was warn the inmate to "calm down" or "watch it" during visits. He hadn't even been warned.

After speaking with his counselor, case manager and various other staff members, his worries were significantly eased. Everybody that he consulted voiced the same opinion- that "engaging in sexual acts" was an excessive charge and overreaching for the offense, and that he probably had nothing to worry about. He'd been experiencing the same spiritual attacks from brothers that Rob had, but this seemed like an extra, greater one. Because of his natural gift- which was his way with words- he had been the primary mouthpiece for the love movement, and this was the only thing he could use to reason and rationalize this latest turn of events.

He got called to the lieutenant's office days later, and he presumed it was the D.H.O. (disciplinary hearing officer) ready to hear his shot. He said a quick prayer on the way over, and he was confident that God was going to show up for him and would get it thrown out. Instead, the D.H.O. officer found him guilty and slammed him- took 27 days of his good time (which pushed his release date back), and took his visits for six months. Baron was stunned. He was numb. The attacks made sense. ..but this didn't.

He was supposed to return to Workcor, but he didn't even consider it. He couldn't even think straight. All of those years in West Virginia so far away- but he had finally made it close to home... then this. He started towards the yard, and hoped Rob was out there. He was the only other person that knew about all of the ttacks and opposition they'd experienced and why. He was the only person who could possibly help him make sense of this latest trial.

He found Rob on the yard, and they walked to a secluded corner. Rob proceeded to minister the co-crucifixion to Baron as gently as he could. Baron knelt and listened. A solitary tear streaked down his cheek as the pressure and full gravity of their position weighed on him. Since he'd been walking with Jesus, he had never experienced so much conflict and had so much gone wrong. He'd never heard God's voice so clearly before, though, or represented Him so boldly. This was evidently the price, but he couldn't help but feel like he had brought all of this mess on himself. Like it all started when he stepped out there and opened his big mouth.

By the time Baron returned to work, his supervisor was enraged that he hadn't reported back immediately after leaving the lieutenant's office. He was fired and written up again. He had supported himself by working in Workcor for the past five years, but now he had managed to lose both his visits and job in the same day. He felt like he was going down- hard and fast.

Two days later, Baron and Rob met on the yard in the evening. Baron felt weak in the spirit, and asked Rob to pray for him. Rob laid his hands on Baron, and prayed that God would impart in his brother what He'd imparted in him. He could sense that Baron had not received the full volume of the co-crucifixion revelation, and the decision he needed to make in light of it. He knew because it eliminated the fear of death by making you look it in the eye and accept it. He knew because once the decision was made, it was liberating and empowering. In the spirit of the prophet Elijah, Rob prayed for heavenly fire to consume his brother's spirit. It did.

About twenty minutes later, filled with the Holy Spirit, Baron's voice went hoarse as he exclaimed his determination and resolve to proceed through the fire- through the furnace of affliction! N matter the trial, regardless of the tribulations- he vowed to do God's will in the midst of the flames- despite the pain. He reviled Satan and his dark forces, and reaffirmed his allegiance to the kingdom of God. When he went back inside, he went straight to his cell. His spirit was overwhelmed. It was dark outside, and he cut the light off and dropped to his knees. He began praying aloud, but for some reasoned, for the first time his words seemed strangely hollow, distant and insufficient. His spirit yearned for more; for more than his mind or soul could express. He felt the urge to let his lips loose, and allow whatever came out of them to flow. He spoke in tongues for the first time, and he didn't stop until he was covered in sweat and out of breath.

"I indeed baptize you with water unto repentance, but He who is coming after me is mightier than I, whose sandals I am not worthy to carry. He will baptize you with the Holy Spirit and fire." (Matthew 3:11)

CHAPTER 28

"THE FIERY TRIAL OF THE SAINTS"

> *. . . the whole world lies under the sway of the wicked one. (l John 5:19)*

> *. . .that He might deliver us from this present evil world. . .(Galatians 1:4)*

> *Beloved, do not think it strange concerning the fiery trial which is to try you, as though some strange thing happened to you. . .(1 Peter 4:12)*

The kingdom of Satan is the current spiritual world power of the earth. He has reigned, through the hearts of men, since the fall of mankind. Satan, along with his evil host, actually police their kingdom (i.e. this world).

> *. . . and the Lord said to Satan, " From where do you come?" So Satan answered the Lord and said, "From going to and fro on the earth, and from walking back and forth on it." (Job 1:7)*

Satan was "going to and fro," and "walking back and forth" policing the earth, the same way officers patrol our streets and communities to ensure that the laws of the land are observe Then, God brings up Job to the devil.

Then the Lord said to Satan, "Have you considered my servant Job, that there is none like him on the earth, a blameless and upright man, one who fears God and shuns evil?" (Job 1:8)

Fearing God and shunning evil are God's commandments- laws of His kingdom. That means they are contrary to Satan's laws. Job was God's man, and his heart was for God's kingdom. That's why God brought him up. He was showing him off; bragging on him. In essence, God was highlighting the fact that Job was in the devil's kingdom, but breaking all of his laws by abiding by God's. So, the devil brings up charges against Job- God's elect- just the same as man's government would if a man broke one of their laws.

So Satan answered the Lord and said, "Does Job fear God for nothing? Have you not made a hedge around him, around his household, and around all that he has on every side? You have blessed the work of his hands, and his possessions have increased in the land." (Job 2: 9, 10)

These initial charges, just like legal ones when first filed, have not been proven. The devil has simply shown "reasonable doubt" that Job's adherence to God's laws was superficial- based solely on God's blessings- and therefore disingenuous and fraudulent. This is an area the devil specializes in- accusing us.

Then he showed me Joshua the high priest standing before the Angel of the Lord, and Satan standing at his right hand to oppose (or accuse) him. (Zechariah 3:1)

Then I heard a loud voice saying in heaven, "Now salvation, and strength, and the kingdom of our God, and the power of His Christ have

come, for the accuser of our brethren, who
accused them before our God day and night,
has been cast down." (Revelation 12:10)

After Satan brought these charges/accusations against Job, his
trial began.

"But now, stretch out your hand and touch all
that he has, and he will surely curse you to your
face!" The Lord said to Satan, "Behold, all that
he has is in your power; only do not lay a hand
on his person." So Satan went out from the
presence of the Lord. (Job 1:11, 12)

The same goes for all of the saints, or the men and women who
live their lives according to God's standard of righteousness. (Rev.
12:17) By abiding by God's laws, we are automatically breaking
the devil's. Then, God brags on us. Then, the devil brings his
charges/accusations and our trials begin. The severity of the trial
depends on the degree of righteousness the devil is sent to "try."
In other words, if your walk is mediocre and lukewarm, you're
not substantially violating Satan's kingdom, and you warrant no
serious attention. We see this reflected in the different degrees of
misdemeanor and felony charges in our legal system. Job's trial
was so severe because he was blameless and upright (or in the
KJV- perfect).

We also see, from verse eleven and twelve, that Satan actually
asked permission. God gave Satan power according to His will.
The entire scenario was ordained and orchestrated by God
Almighty (YHWH). When God originally brought Job up, it was
with a loaded question. The devil was provoked, and could do no
more than what God allowed. God set the boundaries in Job's
trial. Satan carried it out, but it was all purposed and overseen by
our sovereign Lord. Likewise, our trials emanate from the spirit

realm, and the devil can never do any more to God's people than what God allows him to do. When we serve God, He holds the power and authority over our lives. We give it to Him through our faithful obedience and willing subjection to His kingdom. The rest of the first chapter of Job details Satan's attack (i.e. Job's trial). He's robbed of his livestock, his sheep are burned, and all of his kids are killed in a terrible "accident" when the house they were eating in collapsed. Through all of this, Job remained faithful.

> *Job did not sin nor charge God with wrong. (Job 1:22)*

The second attack was also initiated by God. He brags on Job's sustained righteousness and faithfulness, and new charges and accusations fly.

> *Then the Lord said to Satan, "Have you considered My servant Job, that there is none like him on earth, a blameless and upright man, and one who fears God and shuns evil? And still he holds fast to his integrity, although you incited Me against him, to destroy him without cause." So Satan answered the Lord and said, "Skin for skin! Yes, all that a man has he will give for his life. But stretch out your hand now, and touch his bone and his flesh, and he will surely curse you to your face!" And the Lord said to Satan, "Behold, he is in your hand, but spare his life." (Job 2:3-6)*

This time, God allowed Satan to go one step further and attack Job's physical body. Still, He didn't allow the devil to take Job's life. That was never God's purpose. It may be a hard pill to swallow, but the fact of the matter is that God knows all, and even the trials of His saints are ordained by His hand.

The verdict of any trial is the outcome- whether you are found guilty or innocent of the charges that were brought against you. In spiritual trials, your verdict lies in the effect the trial produces in you. If Job had turned from God and cursed Him then he would have been guilty of the charges the devil had brought against him. Instead, in the last chapter of the book of Job, we find Job acquitted and blessed abundantly for faithfully overcoming the vicious trial he faced. God's plan and purposes toward us are always good, and it was always His intent to reward Job's faithfulness. The catch, or clause, in God's design was that the only way for Job to fully establish God's purpose in his life (which was to double everything that he had) was to survive and overcome his trial with his integrity and faith in God intact.

The Lord restored Job's losses when he prayed for his friends. Indeed the Lord gave Job twice as much as he had had before.

Then all his brothers, all his sisters, and all those who had been his acquaintances before, came to him and ate food with him in his house. They consoled him and comforted him for all the adversity that the Lord had brought upon him. Each one gave him a piece of silver and each a ring of gold. Now the Lord blessed the latter days of Job more than his beginning; for he had fourteen thousand sheep, six thousand camels, one thousand yoke of oxen, and one thousand female donkeys. He also had seven sons and three daughters. He called the name of the first Jeminah, the name of the second Keziah, and the name of the third Keren-Happuch. In all the land were found no women as beautiful as the daughters of Job; and their father gave them an inheritance among their brothers. After this, Job lived one hundred and forty years, and saw his children and grandchildren for four generations. (Job 42:11-16)

If you through your fruits live for the evil one then you are a subject of his kingdom. The hardships you encounter are a result of living a life separated from your Creator. If you have obtained riches or glory Satan has given them to you in exchange for your soul. On the other hand, if your evidence reflects God then you are a subject of His kingdom. Albeit, still living in a world dominated by Satan. The trials and tribulations appear identical because the adversary remains the same, but they are completely different in nature and intent.

Because Job was a man of God, God was the source of his calamity. The devil was simply a part of God's "hand." (Job 1:11 and 2:5) We see in chapter forty-two verse eleven that "Job was consoled and comforted for all the adversity that the Lord had brought upon him." There was no mention of the devil because he was merely a tool. If you serve God, no matter how horrible the trial, it is paramount and imperative that you recognize it is of God. You must remain steadfast, patient, and faithful. Overcome the trial and prove the devil a liar. Then watch your blessings multiply accordingly.

"And let us not grow weary while doing well, for in due season we shall reap if we do not lose heart." (Galatians 6:9)

CHAPTER 29

The night had finally arrived~ the love service was ready to begin. All of the choir members and ushers gathered in the chapel, as they do every Sunday evening, around 5:30 p.m. The twelve were present as well. The Protestant church service began at 6:30 p.m. The choir practiced the songs they had planned to sing, and everybody else mingled and fellowshipped. Rob and Baron did not know what to expect. They only knew one thing- that they had been, and were being, obedient.

They had identified a prevalent condition throughout the body of Christ (as a whole). Brothers and sisters whose intentions were good and who genuinely loved God, but could not hear His voice. This led many to seek to serve and please God according to their minds; according to what they "figured" He wanted them to do. Some of the biggest impediments in God's kingdom and Christ's church were members of His body who were being unwittingly used by the enemy. Due to their inability to hear God, the enemy took advantage of their "good intentions" and produced wayward or ineffective ministries, false doctrines and vain traditions. Baron and Rob had been trained by the Holy Spirit to hear God's voice, and their conviction that night was rooted in the commands they'd received.

The head usher called for everybody to gather at the front of the chapel to pray for and over the service. They all locked hands and petitioned God- with heartfelt devotion- to be present that evening and to use them. Right after they finished the chaplain entered the chapel and approached the group with an uneasy countenance.

"Hey- um- guys, there was an incident, and they're talking about locking the prison down. Nothing is official yet. I don't think they're sure what they're going do. So, all we can do is pray about it. I'll let ya'll know something as soon as they tell me," he said, and then he made his way back out the main chapel towards his office.

Baron immediately started to assemble the twelve. He, and the rest of the spiritually sensitive brothers, knew exactly what was going on. It was clear as day. The enemy had been relentless since they began- disrupting, frustrating, and attacking. He was obviously trying to stop this move of God, and through different doorways he had managed to produce much confusion from within. Numerous meetings with the twelve had been unproductive (and sometimes counter-productive) due to disputes of one sort or another. Many of the original twelve had defected, and their slots filled by other brothers. All of these "growing pains" seemed to have been efforts by the enemy to thwart their commission, but they had all failed. Since they wouldn't be stopped from within, this was the enemy's last attempt at stopping them from the outside. Some unclean spirits had incited a brawl on the yard- a half an hour before the service!

The twelve linked in a circle, hands-to-shoulders, and prayed against the enemy and his plot. Two groups split off, then. One went to the chaplain's office, and the other stayed in the main chapel. Both groups waged war in the spirit, and prayed that the service would go forward as planned. About twenty minutes later, the chaplain received the official word: there would be no inmate movement on the compound that night...except a one-way move to church! The chapel erupted in praise! The victory was personal, direct, and oh' so sweet.

Once the chapel move was completed, the chaplain announced to the congregation that every man in attendance that night was absolutely, definitely there for a divine purpose. After the choir selection and a beautiful poem entitled "Brotherly Love" was read, the chaplain preached the meat of the love message they had been given. Then, he called Baron to the pulpit. Baron prayed first- for the congregation and himself- then began.

"I Am has sent me to you with a word. First, I need to see if we are all on the same page. Raise your hand if you are seeking God's power in your life," he said, then raised his own right hand. Every man in the chapel raised his hand as well. "Alright then, turn with me in your Bibles to the book of Luke chapter seventeen," he instructed, then waited a moment for the congregation to find it. "I'm going to be reading verses twenty and twenty- one.

"Now when He was asked by the Pharisees when the kingdom of God would come, He answered them and said, the kingdom of God does not come with observation; nor will they say, 'See here! ' or 'See there! ' For indeed, the kingdom of God is within you. Now, remember that: the kingdom of God is within you, and within me. So when I separate myself from my brothers- from one of you- then I'm separating myself from the kingdom of God within you. So, the next question is: who is my brother?

"For years I was on my Christian motorcycle. Just me, myself and I, and the few brothers I chose to associate with. I'll be the first to confess that for years of my walk I was antisocial, and if you didn't agree with the way that I saw and perceived Scriptures I'd quickly discard you; not see you as my brother; and not even speak to you anymore unless I had to. God has shown me that I was in error

Let's turn to 1 John, chapter four and verse fifteen," he instructed, and then waited again for the congregation to locate the scripture.

"It reads, 'Whoever confesses that Jesus is the Son of God, God abides in him, and he in God'. So . . . now we see what makes you my brother. You don't have to agree with me about everything, or perceive all of the scriptures in the same light as I do. It's your confession that Jesus is the Son of God that allows God- my heavenly Father- to abide in you. That's what makes you my brother! If we continue to allow ourselves to be separated for any other reason- race, nationality, gangs, or doctrine- we are wrong, brothers! Jesus commanded us to love one another, because love is the power source of God's kingdom. Let's turn to one more scripture: Matthew 11:27." He waited a moment, then proceeded to read, "All things have been delivered to Me by My Father, and no one knows the Son except the Father. Nor does anyone know the Father except the Son, and the one to whom the Son wills to reveal Him."

"We see here that if Jesus was unveiled to you, that's because the Father revealed Him to you. He didn't give His Son to us- His love to us- for us to hold onto it. He gave us His love so that we could keep on giving it.

"When we received Jesus into our hearts, we received the Father's love. Jesus was the Father's love. When you received Jesus you received God's kingdom in your heart. But what is the power of God's kingdom? God's love! Jesus is God's love, and God's love is His power! God's power is His love! We've been worrying about everything else, and that's why we've been powerless. We lack power because we lack love! Our love is our power! Our power is our love! Now, turn to three of your brothers right now and tell em'- 'You're my brother, and I love you!'"

The entire congregation exchanged "I love you's" as Baron nodded his approval. He, then, called Rob to the podium. Neither one of them had prepared what they were going to say because they both trusted the Holy Spirit to guide them. Rob did wonder how he was going to get the church involved in its own spiritual deliverance. The twelve had stood the entire service, encircled around the congregation warring in the Spirit against the spirit that had kept the body at Butner from loving freely.They had laid the groundwork in the Spirit, the Chaplain and Baron had provided the teaching and prepared their hearts, and now Rob had to finish the job!

"Praise the Lord, church! Praise the Lord, church! Praise the Lord!" Rob exclaimed, and the congregation erupted in handclaps and praise.

"Listen!'" he continued. "God is trying to pour His love into your hearts this evening and raise you up. We've got to understand what raised Jesus from the grave. The love of the Father raised the Son from the pits of hell after Jesus took on our sins and condemnation on the cross. If the love of the Father raised Jesus from the grave it can also raise you from the dark situations and circumstances going on in your life. Now, stand to your feet, and allow the love of God to consume your hearts," Rob said, and the congregation rose. "Raise your hands, brothers. Raise your hands and receive God's love!" Rob directed. "Now, let's bow our heads.

"Oh, heavenly Father, in the name of Jesus we come to you humbly as we know how. Father, I decrease that you may increase- right now in the name of Jesus. Father, you know these men. Know their hearts and minds, and everything they're going through. We are here tonight to loose these men in the power of your love. To loose your body and to walk in the power of love.

"Right now, in the name of Jesus, I come against the principalities, powers, and the rulers of darkness of this world who are operating according to the order of Molech! I bind you, in the name of Jesus, and cast you into the bottomless pit of hell! I loose this body from your grasp right now- in the name of Jesus! You have no more authority- no more dominion- in this place! I cast down every imagination and pull down every stronghold that exalts itself against the knowledge of God!

"Now have your way, Father God, in this place. Move, Lord! Move, Holy Spirit! Consume us with your love! Consume us, Father! Oh, thank you, Lord. We receive it, Father. We receive it! Hallelujah! Hallelujah! I seal this petition in the blood of Christ. Now, let the church say victory!" Rob said, shouted and pumped his fist in the air.

"VICTORY!" the church exclaimed.

"Victory!" Rob yelled again.

"VICTORY!" they echoed.

"Victory!" he shouted a third and final time.

"VICTORY!" the church proclaimed, and burst into cheers and praise.

CHAPTER 30

"FAITH, HOPE, LOVE"

These are the three "Kingdom Keys" we desire to leave you with. Since we've expounded on love, we will now shift the focus to the next important key- Faith. While the new-age movement and many other self- seeking philosophies teach the misuse of this key for selfish gain, we perceive that the vast majority of God's people do not comprehend the true intent and context of Jesus' teaching on faith. It is ABSOLUTELY IMPERATIVE that you get this.

> *So Jesus answered and said to them, "Have faith in God. For assuredly I say to you, whoever says to this mountain, 'Be removed and be cast into the sea, ' and does not doubt in his heart, but believes that those things he says will be done, he will have whatever he says. Therefore I say to you, whatever things you ask when you pray, believe that you receive them, and you will have them." (Mark 11:22-24)*

Jesus' quote at the end of verse twenty-two is the beginning of this teaching on faith, and this maxim is the foundation of everything else that followed. Jesus said, "Have faith in God." Jesus never intended to inspire His disciples to believe in themselves.

Man, apart from God, has no supernatural power to control events, outcomes, or his own destiny. If a man gains power by exercising his faith, apart from God, this "power" is a facade and demonic in origin. Power to shape events, circumstances, or alter reality in any way is not based in the natural. It is supernatural. If it is supernatural, then its source is from one of two kingdoms- God's or the devil's.

The rest of the passage expounds on the immense power of faith. However, when Jesus said, "He will have whatever he says" if he "does not doubt in his heart but believes that those things he says will be done," it was still with "faith in God" as the premise. "Whatever things you ask when you pray" should also be based on faith in God. In other words- whatever God says, whatever He reveals (or has revealed) about His will, no matter how outlandish or far-fetched or "unrealistic" it may seem- believe it. And pursue it. And speak it. And pray for it.

Jesus was not teaching His disciples that God would be on standby, at their beck-and-call, ready to serve them and do their bidding if they only "believed." This would present countless conflicting scenarios within the body of a billion-or-so proclaimed believers: like two believers praying and believing in God for two contrasting outcomes. Jesus repeatedly reminded His disciples that His words and works were the Father's and not His own.

"Most assuredly, I say to you, the Son can do nothing of Himself, but what He sees the Father do; for whatever He does, the Son also does in like manner." (John 5:19)

"I can of myself do nothing. As I hear, I judge; and My judgment is righteous, because I do not seek My own will but the will of the Father who sent Me." (John 5:30)

"My doctrine is not Mine, but His who sent Me."
(John 7:16)

"The words that I speak to you I do not speak on my own authority; but the Father who dwells in me does the works." (John 14:10).

"The word which you hear is not Mine but the Father's who sent Me." (John 14:24)

To be as the Master requires the disciple to adopt His approach, and Jesus' primary focus was the Father's will. To believe that God exists to do our will is not having faith in God- it is having faith in ourselves. We must remember that God was not created for us; we were created for God.

The only way to have faith in God is to seek to know Him and His will. Then we can believe in Him. You cannot have faith in something or someone you know nothing about. But once we get to know Him, and we receive a word or sign from Him, we can pray and have faith in what we ask for because we know it is of Him.

But without faith it is impossible to please Him, for he who comes to God must believe that He is, and that He is a rewarder of those who diligently seek Him.(Hebrews 11:6)

We must believe that God is, but also that He rewards those who "diligently seek Him." Those who diligently seek Him find out what His will is for their lives, and they ask accordingly. They are rewarded by receiving those things they ask for. God's will is established in our lives when we ask and believe in God for it. Love is the first key, and it is the actual power. Love must

Baron Stepney and Robert M. Paris

be established for God's supernatural power to filter to and through man.

But faith is the key to access God's love (power). Faith is the vehicle that literally crosses the bridge and retrieves God's power from the spirit realm, then brings it into our physical reality. Power for the believers is sitting right there, waiting in the spirit. Faith is the key. Faith goes and gets it. You must have faith to believe in Jesus. You must have faith to follow Jesus. And all who truly possess faith in God are attracted to Jesus, because He embodies God's love, and faith and love are attracted to each other.

Jesus did not look for anybody to heal- they came to Him! The sick, lame, and needy were drawn to Him. Their faith was all they had. The faith of God within their spirits gravitated to the love of God when it was in their midst and miracles followed. Because when FAITH and LOVE unite, they answer HOPE.

> *Jesus said to her, "Did I not say to you that if you would believe you would see the glory of God?" (John 11:40)*

> *To them God willed to make known what are the riches of the glory of this mystery among the Gentiles: which is Christ in you, the hope of glory. (Colossians 1:27)*

One word was cited three times in the verses above: glory. We hope for glory! Nothing less will suffice. Whether it is a glorious healing, a glorious provision, the glory of Christ reproduced and magnified within us, or the ultimate hope of our glory revealed as sons of God when Jesus returns and we become as He is- our hopes are only obtainable through faith and love. When our faith in God and our love for God are rooted in Christ, then the riches of His glory will be produced.

> *And now abide faith, hope, love, these three; but the greatest of these is love. (Corinthians 13:13)*

EPILOGUE

While every teaching in this book is relevant to your growth and helpful in comprehending your ultimate calling and purpose in God's kingdom, we were moved to urge you to revisit the Love chapter (chapter 22). The importance, pertinence and gravity of love in the life of the believer is immeasurable and without comparison. Without it you will remain powerless and stagnate at best. With it there exist no boundaries or limits to how far God can take you in your walk in Christ.

You can only go as far as your heart will take you. If your heart were a car, then love would be its gas. When you started reading this, your love tank might have been half full (we're giving you the benefit of the doubt!), and now it may be full, but the messed up people and situations you will undoubtedly encounter have the potential to leave you on "E". That's why the twenty second chapter on love is worth multiple readings. Love is the most fundamental aspect of our walk, but it is the hardest attribute to exhibit in a world of darkness.

You may have read this book fairly quickly, but it is a spiritual text and meant to be studied and applied. The speed with which you are able to consume content should be disregarded, as truth must be absorbed and acted on to prove beneficial. We advise you to not jump to 'The Keys to the Kingdom, Book Two: Faith' simply because you can, but rather allow these truths to germinate in your spirit and soul and bear fruit!

We also encourage you to spark conversation based on the fresh revelation (new wine!) you've been introduced to. It is necessary that this new unveiling of God's will and word become widespread to help usher the body of Christ into a higher realm of enlightenment and power in the Spirit. Do your part! Sound your trumpet!

May you continue to bear your cross daily, submit your will, and present yourself a living sacrifice to Him who created you and sent His Son to die for us all! To Him be the kingdom, the power, and the glory- forever and ever!

Hallelujah! Hallelujah! Hallelujah!

Printed in the United States
By Bookmasters